HEAL YOUR BROKEN HEART

HEAL YOUR BROKEN HEART

Michael Kane

White Cloud Blue Sky Publishing
2012 Los Angeles • California

ISBN-13: 978-0-9851892-0-4
ISBN-10: 0-985189-20-7
Publisher's Address: 5150 Wilshire Blvd. Suite 507
Year of publication: 2012
Library of Congress Control Number 2012948645

For all of us who have ever suffered from a broken heart.

Acknowledgments

My gratitude and deepest thanks go to the following people, who each brought their unique gifts to the creation of this book.

Michael Devin and MaryAnn Daniel, whose feedback on early drafts was invaluable.

Daria Di Benedetto who spent many hours with me discussing and fine-tuning the text. Her willingness to help was both generous and constant, and I deeply appreciate all that she gave to the realization of this book.

Christy Walker whose skills as a copy editor were only surpassed by her excitement about the book, and without whose efforts the text would not read as fluidly as it does.

Casey Kringlen for inspiring the book cover, and for his proofreading skills along with those of Sean Hemeon, Antony Barr, Angela Allen-Barr and Nigel Sampson. Who would have thought proofreading could be so much fun?

To the late and beloved Marilynn Lovell Matz who lit a lantern for me many years ago and helped me find my way out of the darkness. She taught me more about love and myself than I had thought possible.

David Phelps, my partner for life, who suggested I write this book and then with surgically focused critiques helped me see what I was overlooking. His input has not only made this book what it is, he made me a better teacher in the process.

And to everyone who participated in the Heal Your Broken Heart workshops, thank you for sharing your stories and having the courage to heal your broken heart.

Table of Contents

Introduction _____

YOUR HEART HAS been broken. Someone you love has changed the course of your life by telling you what you never wanted to hear: that your relationship is over. In the cold aftermath of those incomprehensible words, you're tied in knots and emotionally exhausted. Your resulting pain can make you feel hopeless, unwanted, unlovable and alone. You may believe in this moment that you will never be loved again and that love itself is not worth the effort. Although your broken heart is producing these and other devastating feelings, I want you to know that your situation is not hopeless, you are worthy of love and love most definitely *is* worth the effort.

As a result of your heartache, you may choose to isolate yourself—but you are far from alone. At this moment you stand with millions of people who suffer from a broken heart. Some of these hearts are newly broken; others have been broken for months or even years. The universally shared experience of the unyielding pain of a broken heart is undeniable.

Our deepest understanding of love comes from our internal connection to it. When this internal connection is interrupted, severed through emotional trauma, blocked or shut down, our relationship to love suffers, and consequently, we suffer. The heart is the center of love, the core of our being. It is the internal abode where we feel the beauty, simplicity and sweetness of love, the place inside each of us where love is experienced in its most sublime and powerful form.

The heart can be broken in an instant by the cleanest of cuts, by the harshest of actions or by years of small continuous indifferences that eat away at our sense of self and our belief in love. When we hurt, we want our pain to go away, and it's natural to long for a swift solution to our heartache. But where the heart is concerned, a one-shot, silver bullet approach would be the ultimate disservice. Instead of a quick fix, we will follow a slower, reliable and effective path that will honor your pain and allow you to recover from it.

If your heart was recently broken, going through the process in *Heal Your Broken Heart* makes perfect sense—but what if you want to heal from a heart that was broken years ago? Can this book help you, too? Yes, it can, although you might wonder if it's wise to open up those old wounds and feel all that pain again. It might sound like the last thing you would ever want to do, but connecting to your historical heartache is one of the best personal health choices you can make, and for this important reason: Although heartache changes as it ages, it doesn't completely go away without our conscious involvement to remove it. Heartache feels different during the first days, weeks and months than it does a year or two later. As time passes we do feel better because time distances us from the initial shock of our broken heart. But what time alone can never do is remove our core heart wounding. Whatever is at the center of our heartache sits inside of us, regardless of how much time has passed. We may gain distance from the initial trauma of a broken heart, but our core wounding remains; it doesn't evolve into something else. From this perspective, it makes sense to acknowledge, understand and release our pain, so we can replace it with something far better. That something is love.

This book is about love. Love is what will heal you. Not love from the person who broke your heart, but love from within yourself.

My interest in issues of the heart dates back well over 35 years, but it took a particularly fascinating turn in the mid-1990s when I began developing the Heal Your Broken Heart workshop. This workshop was my response to the quiet pandemic of broken hearts I saw in the world around me. So many people I spoke to were suffering unnecessarily from heartache that I was moved to do something on a larger scale than I could in my private practice as a life consultant. I believed that what I'd discovered, both through my own healing and helping my clients heal, would translate to other people who were also suffering from a broken heart. This assumption turned out to be correct.

No matter the setting or what the backgrounds and stories of workshop members were, the topic itself placed everyone in a uniquely intimate relationship to their own pain and to the pain of everyone else in the room. The more we learned about each other's heartache, the more we understood our own.

Both the Heal Your Broken Heart workshops and this book are built on the premise that broken hearts are a universally shared experience few of us heal from properly. This means we carry the residue of past wounding with us, making any new heartache hurt that much more. Every time you've had your heart broken, you've been presented with an opportunity to heal. Did you jump at that opportunity? If you're like most of us, you didn't. After all, you were busy dealing with your pain. Before long, your friends and family—and perhaps you—felt you'd suffered enough and it was time for you to get on with your life. You may have felt guilty or selfish for still talking about your broken heart, so instead of living what you were feeling, you got up, brushed yourself off and jumped back into life with a facsimile of a smile on your face—only you were still hurting.

That pain has not gone away. You've simply grown accustomed to it by assimilating it into your "current you."

Pain, in a word, hurts, and at the moment you may feel like running from it. Resist that urge. Take a deep breath and stay where you are, because the solution to what is hurting you is held within the problem. Believe it or not, tucked away in the recesses of your heartache is the information you need to heal your broken heart. Excavating that information and showing you what to do with it is the work we will do together. You'll learn how to recover from what is hurting you, gain a deeper understanding of yourself in the process and feel safe enough to open your heart again.

Dedicate the coming weeks to healing your broken heart. Make this a priority. You are worth it and your future relationships are worth it. The path of this healing will take you to the core of your heart, to the center of yourself. When you arrive at that most sublime and joyful place, you will not be disappointed. You'll marvel at what is held so naturally within you. It's a discovery that is perhaps beyond words, but it is *through* words that you'll reach your goal. My words in combination with yours will take you there. Together, we will speak the language of the heart, and in the process, you will learn what I have learned: Every broken heart is asking to be healed.

Having a broken heart changes you.
Healing a broken heart changes you more.

Using This Book

Everyone who has participated in the development of this process, whether through the workshops or by sitting with me privately, believed that no one could feel as they felt—just like you. But no matter his or her age, background or personal situation, each of these people suffered from a broken heart. Their individual heartbreak made them more like one another than not, and more like you than you might imagine. What helped them can help you.

Before we begin, let's go over a few details about the book that will show you how to get the most out of each phase.

Healing Center

One of the most important tools in *Heal Your Broken Heart* is the creation of a Healing Center. A Healing Center is an area you set aside in your home that is specifically dedicated to your personal healing. It's a place for you to work, put up exercises from the book, post heart-pertinent information and display other visual treasures. Spending time in your Healing Center will help ground and support you, keep you focused and let you see the progress you're making. I'll make suggestions of what to put in your Healing Center as we progress through the 10 phases, and you can add anything else you like. You won't know how powerful it can be to create a Healing Center until you actually do it, but I guarantee that if you put in the effort, you'll be uniquely informed and inspired by the outcome.

The main component of your Healing Center is an area where you can tape or tack things up. If you have some wall space for this, that would work well, or you could use a piece of corkboard, cardboard, foam core or plywood—anything you can tape or pin paper to. A good size would be 4-feet wide by 3-feet high, but you could go either smaller or even larger if you prefer. Do what works best for you.

Incorporating a writing surface like a table or some desk space where you can work through the exercises in each phase is ideal, but not absolutely necessary. Make your Healing Center as special as you can. Dress it up or keep it simple, you decide. There are no limits to what you can do.

Your Healing Center will be in place for several months, so try to put it where it won't be disturbed. If you don't live alone, let your household know that your Healing Center is private. Setting this boundary lets others understand that you're serious about this work. If you don't have the physical space for a Healing Center, you could incorporate it into the Heart Journal you'll learn about in the next section. But if possible, do the full-blown, three-dimensional version of the Healing Center. You won't regret it!

Writing and Your Heart Journal

The more you write about your broken heart, the more you'll understand it. There are over 50 written exercises in this book, most in the form of questions and answers (Q&As). By doing the Q&As, you'll learn what you've only partially known, or perhaps not known at all, about yourself, your broken heart and your relationship to love. This personal insight will be invaluable to you.

If you're unaccustomed to writing, or feel nervous about answering personal questions, keep two points in mind. One, our written exercises are not tests. They're designed to help you understand more about yourself and your broken heart. And two, unless you choose to show your answers to someone, no one but you will ever read them. Grammar, spelling and punctuation are not important. Write down what comes to you and don't edit your answers. Focus on getting your thoughts out of your head and onto paper. Relax and let yourself become accustomed to writing about your heartache.

Minimal space is provided to complete many of the exercises so I recommend creating a Heart Journal to use for all the exercises. It's important to give yourself enough page space to fully express yourself. You'll be surprised at how much you have to say about your broken heart. If you're comfortable writing in longhand, you could use a standard spiral notebook, a blank-page journal or even a legal pad for your Heart Journal. Using a computer is also a reasonable option if that works best for you. Whichever format you choose, make your Heart Journal special to you.

Throughout the book you'll be prompted to place specific exercises in your Healing Center after completing them in your Heart Journal. Make a separate copy of these key exercises by handwriting them on 3x5 cards or any kind of paper you like. They will provide you with both a visual record of your progress and a sort of healing kiosk that will keep your work focused and on track.

Emotions

Emotions are part of life, and they are certainly part of having a broken heart. We'll talk about, and work directly with, the many emotions that are triggered by heartache. Even when we're not discussing emotions per se, you may still feel emotional. Much of this is not predictable, but it is important to let yourself feel what you feel. There may be days when new emotions unexpectedly surface, not obviously related to what you've been reading. This is part of the healing process. Whatever comes up is ready to be looked at and worked through. Every emotion you have, no matter how uncomfortable it makes you feel, will contribute to your healing.

Time

How quickly you progress through the book depends not only on the amount of time and effort you devote to the work, but also on how long it takes you to process and apply what you learn. I usually suggest doing one phase per week, but you may find you want to move through the material at a different pace. There is no right or wrong to this, although I don't recommend rushing through the material.

Time is precious and you deserve the time it takes to heal your broken heart. Even with your busy schedule, finding the time to heal your heartache makes sense. You'll spend more hours mediating your pain than you'll ever need to heal it. Give yourself twenty minutes a day to work on healing your heart. This is time invested in you and right now, you are what counts.

Gender Pronouns

This book is about you, but we can't talk about healing your heart without mentioning your ex from time to time. Since there is no way of me knowing your ex's gender, this fact presents a particular stylistic problem when it comes to gender pronouns. Only referring to your ex as "your ex" was cumbersome, and it felt awkward to continually use the "he or she, him or her" format, standard as it is. I wanted something more streamlined. After trying several variations, I chose to use he/she, him/her, and his/hers. For example, if your ex is male, when you read the following sentence read the "he" and ignore the "she." I've used italics in this example for emphasis:

> Ask from a partner what *he*/she can provide, not what *he*/she will never be able to give you.

Once you become accustomed to this stylistic choice, I think you'll barely notice it.

Phase Endings

Each phase ends with two easy-to-use sections. The first, *Taking Stock,* is a place to organize your thoughts and feelings as you work through the book. The second, *Exercise Review,* lets you track the exercises you'll be working on from phase to phase. Both sections work symbiotically to support and inform your healing.

The streamlined structure of *Heal Your Broken Heart* will help you process your heartache in a logical sequence that will keep you both focused and motivated. All you need to begin is a desire to heal. If you're committed to feeling better, there is nothing that can stand in the way of your progress. You *can* heal your broken heart. There is no doubt. Let's begin!

Phase One

Every broken heart is asking to be healed.

WHEN YOUR HEART is broken, everything changes. Nothing feels the same. Emotions you haven't had for years come crashing into your life like old enemies you'd hoped never to see again. Feelings of betrayal, resentment, abandonment and rage grab hold of you and tear you apart. You might feel victimized by your ex, even though you usually don't think of yourself as a victim.

As part of our work together we will respect, not criticize, your current emotional turmoil. Thinking that you are weak or crazy for having a reasonable response to what you've been through is not only counterproductive and counterintuitive, it's downright counter-*you*. In time you *will* feel better, but right now, there is no way you could feel anything other than miserable because SOMEONE BROKE YOUR HEART! There is no shame in that, but there is more than enough pain in it.

One of our goals is to diminish, and ultimately eliminate, your pain. We'll begin that process with your signing the following Statement of Acknowledgment, which affirms two important facts: one, that your heart has been broken, and two, that you want to heal it.

By signing the Statement of Acknowledgment, you take formal ownership of your healing, a gesture that places you squarely on the path to heal your broken heart.

Statement of Acknowledgement

My heart has been broken, and I truly want to heal it.

_____Date:_____

Congratulations, you've just affirmed the truth about your broken heart and taken personal ownership of your healing. From this self-empowering starting point, we can begin. Let's get to work.

A broken heart left unattended remains broken.

It Hurts

I rarely meet anyone who hasn't had his or her heart broken at least once. Many of us have lost count of the number of times our heart has been broken. Regardless of the circumstances that led to our broken heart, the end result is the same: We hurt. We might hurt more one minute than the next, but the sum of what we feel is pain.

While the first seismic shock of a broken heart is devastating, it's what happens in the weeks and months after the initial life-altering "it's over" news that can do the real damage. Heart pain is systemic. It seeps into every corner of our being, affecting our quality of life, self-worth and what we believe about love. Pain never speaks a nurturing, enlightened or hopeful word. Its mantra is that of limitation, suffering and hopelessness. A broken heart can make us believe false truths about ourselves, convince us we are meant to suffer and persuade us that there is nothing we can do to diminish our pain.

More than anything, we want our pain to instantly go away—but that won't help us heal. Allowing ourselves to feel the depth of our pain is the better path to take. The thought of feeling the full impact of how much we're hurting can sound like a really bad idea. Most of us believe we'll be crushed under the weight of our sorrow if we completely open up to it. We're concerned enough about this that we run from our pain by either denying it or by self-medicating. It's not until we are able to sit with how we feel that we can learn to move through, and ultimately beyond, what is hurting us. In this phase you'll learn a technique for doing just that.

Get Out Your Heart Journal

You may think you know *exactly* how you feel right now, but there is more going on for you emotionally than you realize. Learning all you can about your emotions will let you see exactly what you're dealing with and provide you with a clear path to healing your broken heart.

Being completely honest about how you feel is vital to your recovery. Think for a moment of your emotional pain as a cut filled with dirt. Would you leave a wound like that without cleaning it? Of course not, even though you know that getting the dirt out is going to sting. A dirty wound won't heal properly. It needs to be cleaned. That's basic first aid. Your heart requires and deserves the same practical attention. It needs some good, old-fashioned first aid. Looking your pain in the face is the beginning of our first aid treatment for your heart. We'll start that work now by having you write about what your broken heart feels like.

No one will be hurt by what you are about to write. Allow yourself to express your emotions in writing without fear of judgment, ridicule or reprisal.

Q&A 1.

Describe your reaction to your broken heart. You can write a list of words, phrases or full sentences. Open your Heart Journal and write down whatever comes to mind when you complete the following statement:

My broken heart makes me feel like I've been...

Terrific, you've just successfully completed your first Q&A, but writing about how you feel can take a little practice, so let's keep practicing. Our second Q&A asks for a description of your heart pain. Write what you feel.

Q&A 2.

My heart pain feels like...

You may have used similar language in answering these first two Q&As, which is perfectly fine. It's also perfectly fine if you didn't. Q&As are about discovery—excavating information—not about being right or wrong. There are no wrong answers.

Read through your responses to Q&As 1 and 2, and honor what you've written by not judging any of it. After finishing these two Q&As, one workshop member said: "I didn't know I felt this way. I knew I was hurt, but I'm starting to see there's probably a lot more I don't know about my broken heart." He was right, and you may be feeling the same way.

Acknowledging that your heart is broken allows you to heal.

The next Q&A will show you more of how you've been responding to your broken heart. Don't worry about the number of boxes you check, just try to identify the different emotions you're feeling. When you relate to a word, even slightly, check the box. If you feel neutral, leave the box blank.

Q&A 3.

The following list of emotions covers much of what you've undoubtedly been feeling. Take your time and check the emotions you relate to by completing the statement:

I feel...

☐ abandoned   ☐ astonished

☐ agitated   ☐ bewildered

☐ angry   ☐ bitter

☐ animosity   ☐ confused

☐ anxious   ☐ contempt

☐ apprehensive   ☐ cowardly

☐ ashamed   ☐ crushed

☐ dejected
☐ depressed
☐ despair
☐ desperate
☐ devastated
☐ disappointed
☐ discouraged
☐ disgusted
☐ disheartened
☐ dismal
☐ dispirited
☐ distressed
☐ dreadful
☐ embarrassed
☐ empty
☐ enraged
☐ envious
☐ exhausted
☐ fearful
☐ frustrated
☐ furious
☐ grief
☐ grudging
☐ guilty
☐ hateful
☐ hostile

☐ humiliated
☐ hurt
☐ hysterical
☐ infuriated
☐ insecure
☐ intimidated
☐ irate
☐ irritable
☐ isolated
☐ jealous
☐ lonely
☐ longing
☐ melancholic
☐ miserable
☐ mournful
☐ needy
☐ numb
☐ obsessed
☐ offended
☐ outraged
☐ overwhelmed
☐ panicky
☐ pathetic
☐ petrified
☐ pitiful
☐ possessive

☐ rage   ☐ somber
☐ rejected   ☐ sorrowful
☐ remorseful   ☐ spiteful
☐ resentful   ☐ stressed
☐ resigned   ☐ stupid
☐ sad   ☐ vengeful
☐ selfish   ☐ undesirable
☐ shamed   ☐ unforgiving
☐ shocked   ☐ unwanted

Whether you checked one or all 84 boxes, what you're feeling is real. I've had people check every box and you may have done that too. A broken heart produces a multitude of emotions.

Look over your list. Each of the emotions you've identified with represents a piece of how you've been feeling. Collectively they describe your current emotional state. One of our goals is to help you better understand exactly what is going on inside of you, and this Q&A lets you see the magnitude of what you've been trying to manage emotionally. Seeing the sheer number of emotions you've checked can help you appreciate why you're having trouble getting through your days right now. You're not crazy: you're in pain.

We've arrived at the first of four drawing exercises. You don't have to be an artist to do these exercises—anyone can do them! Like all of the written exercises, these drawings are for you and don't have to be shared with anyone. Each Heart Drawing is another way for you to express your emotions and learn something about yourself in the process.

Heart Drawing No. 1

Find a blank piece of paper of any size, some crayons, colored pencils or markers and get ready to draw how your heart feels today. Use whatever colors you'd like and make the drawing as realistic or as abstract as you want.

Before you begin, sit quietly for a few minutes, focus on your heart and how you feel—then get to work. This drawing is for you, so spend as much time on it as you like. Indulge yourself, express yourself and see what happens.

When you're done, place your first Heart Drawing in your Healing Center.

The heart thrives in the peaceful quiet of self-acceptance.

Setting Up Your Healing Center

This would be the perfect time to set up your Healing Center since you've just done a drawing to put in it! Hopefully you've had a chance to pick a good location, but if not, make that choice now. As a reminder, you're setting up a type of display area. You could use some available wall space or a freestanding piece of corkboard, cardboard, foam core or plywood. Any material you can attach paper to with pushpins, tacks or tape is what we're after.

Your Healing Center will provide you with a dynamic and evolving visual description of your healing as well as give you a comforting place to spend time. Since you've been deeply hurt, comfort is a quality we want to insert into your life every day, and your Healing Center is a great way to ensure that happens. If possible, incorporate a writing surface like a table or desk into your Healing Center so you have a special place to make entries in your Heart Journal.

I hope you come to cherish your Healing Center. It will reflect back to you a clear and loving view of yourself, and allow you to see how much stronger you become as you move through the 10 phases of *Heal Your Broken Heart*.

Can a Broken Heart be Healed?

In these initial phases of your recovery, it's normal to feel as if you're a long way from healing your broken heart. Some people say it feels like they have a mountain to climb. The truth is, you won't feel better until you feel better. Until then, you'll want to trust that healing is possible. I know from experience that by doing this work you can heal your heart, and in the process, you'll learn more about yourself and love.

The path to your healing is through the heart itself. To heal what has been wounded you must go to the center of the wounding. Healing what is an emotional, psychological and spiritual injury is as much a mystical endeavor as a pragmatic one. While many events in our world move us in other directions, love moves us toward a more balanced and meaningful life. Finding what is loving within you— that you are a good, caring and compassionate person—will strengthen your efforts to heal your heart. That you were able to love another person, regardless of the outcome of the relationship, is a testament to your ability to love. There is more love within you and you will share that love again. Trust in this truth.

Let's do our next Q&A.

Q&A 4.

Go back to your list of checked emotions from Q&A 3 and pick seven that feel the most significant to you. If you checked less than seven use the number you have.

Choose a different emotion each day until you complete your list. Spend 10 minutes sitting quietly with the "emotion of the day" and let yourself feel that one emotion. If you have trouble feeling this one specific emotion at the moment you sit down to do this exercise, focus on an incident in your relationship related to it. For example, let's say it's Monday and the emotion you've picked from your list in Q&A 3 is "undesirable." Think of a situation that happened in your relationship that made you feel undesirable. It may have been any number of times your ex wasn't in the mood for sex, or something hurtful that he/she said that caused this emotional response in you. Remembering this will connect you to the emotion it originally evoked.

If your mind wanders during the exercise, and it's likely it will, just bring your focus gently back to feeling the emotion you're working on. Then, in your Heart Journal, write about what you felt. Here are some questions to ask yourself in case you're not exactly sure what to write about. You can add other information of course, but this short questionnaire will get you started:

1. What thoughts came to mind as you felt this emotion today?

2. How did you respond physically—did any of your muscles tighten, did you clench your teeth, did you sigh or did your stomach feel upset, for example?

3. How familiar is this emotion to you? (very, somewhat, not at all.)

4. Can you remember another time in your life when you felt this emotion? If so, describe the circumstances.

5. Did you judge yourself during the exercise?

The benefit of this exercise is that it teaches you how to experience an emotion while you also learn to observe your response to it. Usually we dive into the center of an emotion, react to it and keep reacting to it until it subsides or is replaced by another emotion.

We don't imagine there could be a different way to experience our emotions, but there is. We could pick any emotion to use as an example, but let's say you're feeling unwanted. When this feeling is triggered you fall into the center of it. Unwanted-ness surrounds you. You feel terrible, drag yourself around all day, think some pretty negative thoughts about yourself and annihilate a couple of pints of Häagen-Dazs white chocolate raspberry truffle ice cream. But, if you take another tack and sit with that unwanted feeling, feel all you can feel about it and then write about what that felt like, suddenly you're having a feeling *and* observing how you respond to it.

Once you create this small but significant distance between you and your emotional response, you can ask this important question: *Why do I feel unwanted?* Initially you would say it's because your ex left you, and that would be true, but feeling unwanted—or any other strong emotional reaction you may have—generally doesn't show up in your adult life without having had some earlier incarnation. In other words, your current feeling of being unwanted had a point of origin, an older situation that created it. Perhaps this can help you see that aspects of your current feelings of being unwanted draw on the same feeling you had from an earlier experience, even if it happened years ago. This is part of your core wounding, which was triggered by your breakup. The trigger sets off a chain reaction that heightens your existing emotional response because it draws on the unresolved emotions you have from your past and couples them with what you're feeling now. This doesn't mean your emotions are off, but it does suggest you're feeling new wounding on top of old wounding. This is the major reason why healing properly makes so much sense. If you don't carry unresolved pain forward from this breakup, you won't have to suffer from it in the future because it won't be sitting inside of you waiting to be triggered.

Give yourself the gift of truly healing your broken heart.

Something to Think About

If you let it, pain will teach you about yourself. Suffering isn't a requisite to self-discovery—but when you do suffer and allow yourself to face your pain, you can't help but grow. Listen to your heartache and learn from it; in time it will make you stronger, wiser and more at peace.

The process of healing your broken heart is about understanding and releasing. Acknowledging how you feel makes all the difference. If you feel weak and vulnerable, let yourself feel what you feel and go through these first few phases as slowly as you need to. There is no rush. Healing takes time. Be gentle with yourself, be gentle with your thoughts and be gentle with your heart. In the end, you will succeed.

Taking Stock

In your Heart Journal write about how your heart feels today and describe any specific events, emotional revelations or other relevant information connected to your healing.

Exercise Review

This Phase: • Work daily on the exercise from Q&A 4.

• Add any useful quotes from this phase to your Healing Center.

It's a good idea to finish the majority of the work on Q&A 4 before moving on to Phase Two. Your efforts to understand your emotions now will resonate for you as you move through the book *and* as you move through your life.

Congratulations on committing to *Heal Your Broken Heart*. Your heart will thank you when you're done.

When our heart is broken

We cannot help but realize

That for all the distractions in life,

Our heart truly is

The center

Of our existence.

Phase Two

Your heart holds your personal truth.

YOU KNOW BY how you feel today and from your work in Phase One that you're experiencing some strong emotions. Emotions cause reactions and many of those reactions are reflected in the body, so in this phase we'll look at how your emotional response to your heartache is manifesting physically for you. We'll discover how your spirit has been wounded and what to do about that, and we'll work to release any need you may have to understand your ex's logic.

We'll also write the story of your broken heart. Getting your story out of your head and on to paper is an essential healing exercise that has both short- and long-term benefits. As you write your story, it's likely that new emotions will surface. Expect this to happen, and when it does, remember that there is no reason to feel embarrassed about how you feel—there is no shame in feeling. But first, we'll make an important proclamation about your broken heart.

One Name

Putting your thoughts on paper acts as a conduit to a deeper internal connection. Even writing down a name in the proper context can magnify your commitment to heal. Putting pen to paper brings your focus to whatever you're about to write. The act of picking up a pen or pencil may seem common, but in truth it's a ceremonial gesture, especially if you allow it to be.

Below, write down the name of the person who broke your heart. You obviously know who this is, but naming him or her in the context of this work is an important step in your recovery. You probably think of this name a hundred times a day, but that repetition does little to help you heal. Writing the name down solidifies your commitment to heal and unflinchingly states what happened. This exercise is not meant to place blame; you're simply stating a fact.

Without accusation, finish this statement:

_____ broke my heart.

Read the statement aloud five times. Shout it if you need to! Listen to the sound of the words. Recognize the truth they hold. Remember that this is not about placing blame and only about stating a fact. Well done.

Learn the language of your heart—it will entrance you.

Q&A 5.

I'd like you to write the story of your relationship and especially the details of your breakup. I know this isn't a story that makes you feel good, but writing it down is important. Holding it in takes energy. Freeing up even some of that energy will aid in your healing. Writing produces a different experience for you than talking because writing slows everything down, which will help you remember and process information at a more manageable rate.

Open your Heart Journal, take a deep breath and get to work on writing the story that led to your broken heart. Begin by describing how things were for the two of you when you first got together and go from there. Take as long as you need to tell your story.

For many people this is the hardest Q&A in the book, but it can also be one of the most enlightening ones. The emotional effort required to write down your story will be repaid many times over as you continue this work. If you discovered something new about your relationship by doing this Q&A, describe in your Heart Journal what that was.

As you heal, you are in direct relationship with your inner self.

The Emotional Fetal Position

To love and be loved, we must be open, available and willing to receive. When our heart has been broken, this not only seems like an impossible feat, but a totally undesirable one. What would be the point of opening up, so we could get hurt all over again? Why would we intentionally do something as crazy as that? We feel miserable, freaked-out and used up, so we do what seems to be the only logical thing to do. We slink away, recoil from the world and fold ourselves into the equivalent of an emotional fetal position.

Contracting into an emotional fetal position can be the perfect *temporary* antidote for our heartache. It helps us feel safe and emotionally self-contained when we curl in on ourselves. We protect our heart by keeping it to ourselves and decide when or if we'll let someone in again. But we can run into trouble if we take this reasonable, temporary solution and make it a more permanent one by closing ourselves off from what will heal us. Only love can heal what a lack of love destroyed. The path to opening up to love again happens first within ourselves and then branches out to others, as we feel ready.

Without exception, every person I've met who has been in the throws of a broken heart has been in an emotional fetal position, at least to some degree. Often, you can see it in their posture. Their shoulders are rounded forward, chests sunken and heads slightly lowered. It looks as if they've given up, and in many ways they have. There are internal physical responses, too. We feel a pain in the pit of our stomach, which can eliminate our desire to eat and not eating will quickly affect our energy and state of mind, both of which are already challenged. Sometimes people feel anxious. Their anxiety can keep them awake wasting hours looking at their ex's Facebook status, searching for those all-important changes. The lack of sleep that comes from this type of late-night fixation makes it more challenging for anyone to function normally the following day, which means people's jobs are inevitably impacted.

A more subtle response to an emotional fetal position is the sadness we see in a person's eyes. You would see this same sadness in your eyes if you looked in a mirror right now. In fact, why not do that? Go to a mirror and look into your eyes. Do you see sadness in them? This is nothing to be ashamed of; it's one of the manifestations of your broken heart. The more you heal, the less sadness you will see in your eyes because there will be less sadness in your heart. And, the more you know about what is hurting you, both past and present, the easier it will be for you to heal. The following exercise can help you see some of what you've been through in your life, which will deepen your understanding of yourself and move your healing forward.

It is your right to heal from every broken heart you have sustained.

Quick Draw

How many times has your heart been broken? Take a blank piece of paper and draw a large circle on it to represent your torso. Get a pencil, pen or marker, and draw a heart for every broken heart you've suffered. Think back to when you were a teenager. Many of us sustain our first romantic broken heart that early in the game. Next to each heart write the name of the person you associate with it.

As well as showing you in very clear terms that your heart has been broken more times than you may have realized, this drawing can also help you see, if only by the sheer number of broken hearts you've suffered, that your personal history of broken hearts is probably impacting your life. If you end up with quite a few hearts in your drawing, please don't let it upset you; let it motivate you to heal.

Place this drawing in your Healing Center. It will remind you that the pain you're working through is not imaginary or exaggerated. In the process of healing your most recent broken heart, you're also learning how to heal your historical wounding. Each of the hearts in your drawing represents a profound moment in your life. Every one of those moments should be recognized, named, honored and in time, given the chance to heal. This, you deserve.

A Wounded Spirit

A broken heart wounds our spirit. A wounded spirit colors our view of life. The present looks bleak. The future can look even bleaker. We feel overwhelmed, emotionally ill-equipped, raw and unsure of what to do. When our spirit is wounded it can be hard for us to know exactly how much we're hurting. Many of us mistrust the pain we feel and assume we're overreacting to it. Acknowledging that our pain is real and not imaginary is crucial to the healing process. Our spirit only asks that we be honest about how we feel.

The following multiple-choice Q&A looks at the state of your spirit. Check the boxes that best match how you feel.

Q&A 6.

1. How emotionally stable do you feel right now?

   ☐ very   ☐ somewhat   ☐ not at all

2. How hopeful do you feel about your life in general?

   ☐ very   ☐ somewhat   ☐ not at all

3. How hopeful do you feel about your ability to love again?

   ☐ very   ☐ somewhat   ☐ not at all

4. How hopeful do you feel about your ability *to be* loved again?

   ☐ very   ☐ somewhat   ☐ not at all

5. How possible do you feel it is to recover from your current feelings of loss?

   ☐ very   ☐ somewhat   ☐ not at all

6. How positive do you feel about your relationship future?

   ☐ very   ☐ somewhat   ☐ not at all

7. How positive do you feel about your future in general?

   ☐ very   ☐ somewhat   ☐ not at all

8. How strong does your spirit feel?

   ☐ very   ☐ somewhat   ☐ not at all

The more recently your heart has been broken, the higher the likelihood most or all of your responses were either *not at all* or *somewhat*. If this is true for you, and under the circumstances it would make perfect sense for it to be, please do not judge yourself. This information gives you an overview of the current state of your spirit and lets you know more about how you're feeling. As your heart begins to heal, your spirit will do the same.

People want us to feel better. We want to feel better. There is pressure on all sides for us to be ourselves again. We rush to improve the condition of our heart by acting as if we're fine when we're not. We fake happiness, and our spirit takes the hit from this forgery. No one who cares for you wants to see you hurting, and you certainly don't want to stay with the pain you're feeling a moment longer than necessary. But when you hurt, you hurt. Trying to artificially acceler-ate the rate of your healing, or pretending you're doing better than you are, will not help you heal. While your friends and family may feel better by this show of false progress, you will not.

We generally approach a broken heart as something we should "get over" and "move on" from, not actually heal. When a heart remains broken, the spirit is left unfortified. Healing your broken heart and revitalizing your spirit are accomplished together. One doesn't happen without the other. Since your self-esteem has taken a hit, you're feeling disheartened and you may be questioning a number of things about yourself. This sense of yourself is connected to your spirit.

The healing of your spirit, your sense of hope and your belief in what is positive and possible is also a goal in our work together. Your spirit has been wounded every time your heart has been broken, but it need not stay wounded forever. Each time you are good to yourself, have a loving thought, allow yourself to be who you are and don't judge yourself, you take a significant step in rebuilding your spirit.

The spirit and the heart heal as one.

The Need to Understand

There are reasons people mislead or lie to us, but understanding those reasons is rarely easy. We may never figure them out no matter how much we want to, and this is where we can get bogged down. It might seem that by having a detailed explanation of the ins and outs of our ex's logic we'll discover why he or she did what they did. We believe this inside information will heal us, but it won't. Learning what went on in our ex's head ultimately amounts to hearing a lot of words that have very little meaning to us. Our expectation is that by extracting this information from our ex we'll be freed, released from imagining the worst and given closure. This is rarely, if ever, the outcome.

Holding on to a need to understand your ex's logic will keep you where you are. Releasing it permits you to move forward. If this is an issue for you, this next Q&A gives you the opportunity to explain why this "need to know" is so important to you.

Q&A 7.

Imagine you've just been handed a detailed explanation of how your ex was thinking and reasoning during the final stages of your relationship. Describe how you believe this new information will help you heal:

If you have a burning desire to know what went on inside your ex's head what you just wrote will make perfect sense to you. The concern here is that you want something that: (1), you are highly unlikely to get, and (2), even if you were to get it, would probably only hurt you. Read through your response to Q&A 7, it gives you a perfect description of what you want to release. To assist you with this release, we'll do our First Statement of Release. Once you start releasing what has been holding you back, your burden will lighten and you will begin to feel better.

Fill in your ex's name in the blank below then read the entire statement out loud. Copy the First Statement of Release and put it in your Healing Center then read it often. Regularly repeating its message will help you heal.

First Statement of Release

I release my need to understand _____'s logic in making the choices he/she made that have so profoundly impacted me. In releasing this need, I acknowledge that the information would not help me heal.

Whenever you find yourself going to the place of "needing to know," go to your Healing Center instead, read your First Statement of Release and remember that letting go of this need will help heal your broken heart.

A Note About Music

Do you have a favorite song or artist you associate with your ex? You know, music you once loved that now thrusts you into thoughts of your lost beloved and the melancholic pain connected to your breakup? If you're like most people, you do. You're dealing with enough pain. It's counterproductive to increase your feelings of sadness and loss, especially with something like this where you have some control. Take a proactive stance and stop listening to this music. If you want to hear it once more before you remove it from your life for a while, go ahead. Play it one last time, let yourself feel *really* melancholic and hopefully you'll have a good cry. Then put it away.

Slide that CD into a hidden corner and leave it there for at least a year—seriously, a year. Remember to erase it from your music players and to take it off your computer's hard drive and cloud. Be disciplined about this, it will help you heal.

When you indulge your emotional attachment to the music you associate with your ex, you unintentionally romanticize your pain. You now know that to heal you must face what is hurting you, but romanticizing how you feel will only distract you from achieving a purer understanding of your true emotions.

Hearing any sad song can elicit a similar reaction from you as your favorite relationship song. Pop music, country music and the blues are filled with songs about breaking up. Even classical music has its mournful adagios. One workshop member said, "When I feel like this, it seems like every song I hear is about people breaking up and suffering from a broken heart!" It's wise to buffer yourself from music that can make you feel unnecessarily sad.

Q&A 8.

Formally naming the song or artist you associate with your ex is the first step in removing this music from your life, at least for the next 12 months. Signing off on this agreement commits you to this act of self-protection.

The song or album that causes me pain when I hear it is:

_____

I agree to stop listening to this music for one year.

_____Date:_____

Please don't interpret this as musical deprivation—that you "can't" listen to this music for a year. Instead, recognize that by protecting yourself in this way, you keep yourself from being

unnecessarily hurt. You're giving yourself a gift, not taking something away from yourself. It makes sense to do this. Your heart
knows this to be true.

Listen for the music playing in the deeper regions of your heart.

Something to Think About

Healing is a step-by-step process, and now for you it's a phase-by-
phase one. You're new to this journey, which means patience is
required. It's natural that you want to stop hurting as quickly as
possible, but it's important to remember that you cannot rush through
this work. By taking the time to heal properly, you'll release the pain
you currently feel and gain a new level of self-confidence and personal understanding.

   As you work through the remaining phases, you'll see that some
days will be easier than others, and you'll also see that you are
definitely moving forward. Be patient with yourself, with your
uneven progress and with your need to get it all done quickly.

Taking Stock

In your Heart Journal write about how your heart is feeling. Describe
any new emotional insights you may have had and report other
relevant information that is connected to your healing.

Exercise Review

This Phase: • Repeat the First Statement of Release whenever you
                feel the need.
              • Remove the music you associate with your ex and
                steer clear of other songs that might make you
                overly melancholic.
              • Add any useful quotes from this phase to your
                Healing Center.

Your heart holds the essence of who you are,

The map to where you are going,

And your unfettered and triumphant connection

To love.

Phase Three

Love will replace your pain.

WHY IS IT so hard to change what you're used to doing and allow your emotions to shift? Why do you hold on so tightly to what you've known? Why are you afraid to let go? Is your love for your ex of such a profound nature that letting go of him seems impossible, even crazy? Is it that you can't conceive of living a fulfilling life without her? Are you just plain afraid? Whatever the reason, when you cling to the loss of your ex and succumb to your cravings for him/her, you can't heal. How can you when you're still in a relationship? But instead of being in a relationship with a person, you're in a relationship with your pain. You unintentionally make that pain worse by not letting go. If you want to suffer, keep holding on to what no longer exists. If you want to feel whole again, you'll need to let go. In this phase, you'll build on the releasing work you began in Phase Two. When you know more about what you're holding on to and why you've resisted letting go, releasing becomes possible.

This phase also looks at what you asked of your relationship, why you can get so caught up in wanting to know what went wrong, and the impact your personal history can have on you.

Releasing

Why is it so hard to let go? Why do we hold on so tightly to people and situations we know are not good for us? Why do we listen with feigned interest when our friends tell us we're crazy not to move on? Are we just stubborn and determined to have things go our way? This may be one explanation, but if so, why are we so defiantly bull-headed?

If I were to pick the one thing people do that keeps them repeating the same frustrating and disappointing patterns for years, it would be that they doggedly hold on to what doesn't work for them. They hold on so tightly for so long that it eventually becomes impossible for them to imagine living another way. I've done this in my life, and chances are you've done it, too. You could be doing it right now. Unfortunately, it never works. Releasing, surrendering and setting someone or something free is the path to healing.

If you're holding on to a belief that your ex is going to return, or that you'll be vindicated in some way, you're feeding your pain, nothing more. Remaining in a state of loss-consciousness, where all you think about is what you've lost, keeps you attached to what is no longer there, making it almost impossible for a new and healthier experience to enter your life.

Releasing everything associated with your emotional pain takes time, but it can be done. What you'll discover in the process, contrary to what you may have assumed, is that when you actively release your connection to someone, you aren't left floating alone in a terrifying void. Instead, letting go of what you've clung to allows something better to move in around you. We might call that something love, a feeling of safety or a clearer sense of self. Whatever the name,

how you feel when you let go will surprise you and show you there is
far more good to be found in releasing than in holding on.

Release—let go—surrender your pain.

Q&A 9.

Before you can release anything, you need to know what you're
holding on to. For example, are you resisting letting go of your ex; a
belief about yourself as the "good" girlfriend, boyfriend or spouse; or
the relationship itself, which can include your fear of how people
might view you now that you're single again? Perhaps you're holding
on to all three, and you may certainly be holding on to something
else, too. See if you can name what you would be better off releasing.

I am holding on to:

Put this in your Healing Center, look at it daily, and as you read
through it each time, begin by saying, *I am releasing* _____.

It's true that we'll resist releasing what we've held on to for years,
no matter how unhealthy the person, behaviors or attitudes might be
for us. Even the worst emotional habit can eventually feel like an old
friend. Letting go of a person, a way of thinking or acting, or a
patterned emotional response can feel like we're losing something we
may be afraid to live without. Learning to release allows us to heal.
When we release, we move away from the fear that has motivated us
to cling so tightly to our old way of being. Stepping outside this fear
frees us.

If you find yourself resisting the idea of releasing, be patient with yourself, but keep trying. Once you let go, you'll be surprised at how much lighter and more balanced you feel.

Everyone Has a Past

Some people see a direct connection between their childhood experiences and how they react to situations in their adult lives, others see little or no connection. Perhaps you're familiar with the saying that we are a product of our experiences. We may be more than this, but it's likely that what we saw, heard and felt as children has some influence on what plays out in our adult lives.

Most of us don't survive childhood without sustaining some degree of heart wounding. We carry our early heart wounding with us into our first young adult relationships and it's there that it can resurface. You may have noticed that you partner with people who have the ability to push some of your emotional buttons. While you love the person you're with, he/she can sometimes send you into emotional overdrive with a word, glance or gesture. You spin out because your older wounding has been triggered. One of the advantages of relationships is that they give us the opportunity to heal this type of historical wounding. If we don't know what our historical wounding is and how we react to it, we lose this chance to heal. What do we do instead? We might fight with our lover, partner or spouse, indulge in addictive behaviors, shutdown entirely — or do a combination of all three.

Our wounding is seen in how we react to it. People may not know they've hurt us or that we're hurting, but they do see how we act. For instance, is there something you've heard repeatedly over the years that describes what happens to you when you're in a relationship? Have your exes told you that you can't be intimate, have a temper, have trouble receiving, are selfish and unthinking, like to suffer, love drama, drink too much or use drugs to escape your problems? If you've heard any of these, take note. That description of you paints a picture of how you've reacted to pain. One person saying you're closed off emotionally is one person's opinion. Two or more people saying it starts to sound like a consensus rather than one ex's angry response to a failed relationship.

Our next Q&A will help you learn some of how you've reacted to your historical wounding. As always, please don't judge yourself for your response.

Q&A 10.

Write down what your exes have said to you in the final days of past relationships. In other words, what have you been told about yourself that you may not believe, but you've heard?

Many people see a pattern when they answer this Q&A, and if you did too, think of this as information that can benefit you. The descriptions you wrote down are ways you express pain. In the future you'll be able to function differently in a relationship, but for now we're looking at what has hurt you and how your pain is expressed.

What We Ask of Love

So much of the pain we experience in relationships is a result of what we ask of love. What we ask of love, meaning how we expect love to be expressed to us, is important for us to understand. By learning what we ask of love, we begin to get a look at the bigger picture, which then allows us to develop relationships that are balanced and fulfilling.

We usually don't pause to consider what we ask of love; but when we're in a relationship, we can be thinking about it much of the time. We'll have thoughts like...

- *Why doesn't she know I hate it when she does that? If she really understood me, she wouldn't do it.*

- *He never thinks to bring me a gift just to say he loves me, and I give him little presents all the time.*

- *She knows I want to have more sex—if she really loved me, we'd be having it every day.*

- *He thinks he has every answer, that he's always right, so I never feel like I can offer any suggestions. If he really loved me, wouldn't he want to listen to what I have to say?*

These types of thoughts are representative of how we think love should be expressed to us. This view of love is based on our personal history. We may not see this connection immediately, but it's there.

What we ask of love is not always what love is designed to give. When we ask for what cannot be given, we are easily hurt, and continuing to ask deepens our pain and prevents our heart from healing.

If you felt a lack of love when you were young, we want to be sure that lack is not negatively affecting you now. How can you tell if this is happening? If you ask someone to give you the type of love you didn't receive growing up, you ask that person to provide you with a kind of love he or she is not equipped to give. This stings you twice. Once because you don't get the love you've been missing since childhood, and twice because it feels like your beloved is letting you down. If you knowingly, or unknowingly, have an expectation that your beloved should fill an emotional hole that was created by a lack of maternal, paternal or sibling love, you will forever be disappointed. Ask from a partner what he/she can provide, not what he/she will never be able to give you.

Q&A 11.

In your relationship, did you ask your ex to love you in ways he/she wasn't meant to, or in which he/she was not capable? If so, describe what you asked of, or expected from, him/her.

Learning what you've been asking of love can help you change what you ask of it in the future. While no one you fall in love with will be able to heal your childhood pain, they may be capable of loving you fully, and that you deserve.

If you want to know what love really means to you,
ask your heart.

What the !@$% Happened?

We can spend so much time and energy trying to figure out how everything went wrong in our relationship that we leave little time for the rest of our lives and no time or energy to devote to our healing. Insisting on understanding what happened to us can become a part-time job and a full-time obsession. I've spoken with people who were still talking about the nuances of a relationship that ended three years earlier. That's a long time to keep going over the same material. Most of us don't spend three years trying to understand an ex, but it's normal to want to figure out what went wrong in our relationship. We want to know what our ex was really doing when he said he was on that business trip to Philadelphia. We want to know how it could possibly take her an hour to run out for cigarettes *and* why she thought we believed her in the first place. More importantly, we can't understand how he could love us one day and not the next. We especially want to know that. But there comes a point when wanting to know what happened does nothing more than distract us from our healing.

In the last phase you were asked to release your need to understand your ex's logic, but it's not only your ex's logic you'll probably never understand, it's also his/her emotions, psychological motivations and ability to give and receive love. You may never be given the opportunity to have any of that spelled out for you. All the same, imagine you could know everything that transpired in your ex's mind and heart, do you think that information would make you feel better? Would it help you heal? Would it tell you something truly important that you don't already know? Whether you were with her for three months or fifteen years, you probably thought you knew her better than it turns out you did. Whether it was a secret, faulty communications or the inability to find solutions to your problems that caused the unhinging of your relationship, your work is to discover what happened to *you*, not to your ex.

I understand why you might want to know more about what motivated your ex to make the choices he/she did, but that information will only take you so far. Beyond that, you're left to speculate. Speculation takes time—your time. It leads to theories, perhaps fairly accurate ones, but theories that will be nearly impossible to prove. Do you want to be a relationship theoretician, or would you rather get on with your life?

Whether you're working to release your need to know what happened, or you're stuck on some other issue regarding your ex, you can easily cross the line from general curiosity to more compulsive-like fixations. How do you know if you've crossed the line and become compulsive about your ex? Read the following list. If you relate to any of the nine points, you might want to consider pulling back.

Nine Broken Heart Compulsive Behaviors

1. You constantly check your email to see if there is something from your ex. Perhaps a suggestion that you reconcile, an apology, or a more detailed explanation of what happened.

2. You regularly drive by his/her house, apartment building, or place of work hoping to see him/her. (See Phase Four: Passion Drive-Bys.)

3. You hope that every time you check your voice mail or receive a text message there will be something from your ex.

4. When your phone rings, your heart skips a beat in anticipation that it might be him/her.

5. You have ongoing conversations in your head with or about your ex. (See Phase Five: Internal Monologues.)

6. You can't stop thinking of what you could do or say that would get you and your ex back together.

7. You've started telling your friends that you're doing fine when you definitely are NOT.

8. You find it increasingly difficult to focus on your personal and professional responsibilities because your heartache is so distracting.

9. You have serious thoughts of revenge, thoughts you're afraid you might act upon.

Write down the Nine Broken Heart Compulsive Behaviors you relate to and start to recognize when you're acting on them. Learning to identify when you're about to engage in a self-defeating behavior allows you to make a healthier choice in that moment, and that healthier choice will move your healing forward.

Finding the Truth

In Q&A 5 you told your story by describing the events that resulted in your heart being broken. Your ex probably has a different story of the same events. You each have your own truths. You each have your own pain. Your pain contributes generously to your personal story.

One of pain's many pitfalls is that it creates an incredibly persuasive story. Not that your story is wrong, but perhaps you can see how it's told through your personal filter of pain. The more you think and talk about the story of your broken heart, repeating the same interpretation of events, the more doggedly convinced you'll become of it's sole accuracy. But there were two of you in the relationship, and the story you wrote was written together. Part of healing involves seeing your relationship in a larger framework and gaining a more expansive and inclusive view.

The next four Q&As will help you begin to develop this larger framework or bigger picture perspective. Part of you may resist changing your view, but any work you do to gain more understanding will help heal your broken heart.

Q&A 12.

Give three reasons your relationship didn't work and state them without blame or judgment.

1. _____.

2. _____.

3. _____.

Think of your answers as explanations as to why the relationship dissolved and not as ammunition to use against yourself or your ex.

Q&A 13.

Name three ways you were hurt during the relationship. Again, without blame or judgment.

    1. I was hurt when/because _____.

    2. I was hurt when/because _____.

    3. I was hurt when/because _____.

Your words are an honest description of why you're hurting. This information is probably not new to you, but seeing it written down can be helpful.

Read your responses from Q&A 13 aloud and after each one say:

I want to release the hold this hurt has on me.

When you've finished, close your eyes, sit quietly for several minutes and let your decision to be released from this pain sink in. One of the most powerful tools in the releasing process is your conscious involvement in it. You've just consciously acknowledged your desire to be released from three significant elements of your pain. This has the potential to make a real difference for you.

The heart understands, but does not fear, pain.

Q&A 14.

Now, without blame or judgment, name three ways your ex was hurt during your relationship.

1. _____ was hurt when/because _____.

2. _____ was hurt when/because _____.

3. _____ was hurt when/because _____.

My hope is that there wasn't a lot of pain experienced by you or your ex, but people do get hurt when they become confused about love. None of us loves perfectly, although we can learn to love better.

Q&A 15.

Review your responses from Q&As 13 and 14. Do you see any similarities in the way you and your ex were hurt? If so, describe them.

Looking, if only briefly, from your ex's point of view can help you feel more compassion—not pity—for yourself and your ex. Compassion will make it easier for you to release what has hurt you. The more genuine compassion you come to feel, the clearer you will see your relationship, and that clarity will bring you peace.

Something to Think About

Releasing happens in two stages. The first is when you recognize that you want to let go of someone, a particular behavior or a way of thinking. The second stage evolves over time and involves your processing of what you've agreed to release. Some days you may feel like backtracking, hoping to stop the release you've set in motion. When this happens, reaffirm your commitment to releasing. If you need to repeat any of the exercises in this phase related to releasing, do them again.

That you may occasionally think about reneging on your commitment to release is only natural. To heal successfully is not to move through the process flawlessly, but to understand that the path you are on has curves and can sometimes circle back on itself before it moves forward again. Anticipate changes in how you respond throughout this entire process. Each day will be different. What feels solid in one moment can feel less so in the next. In time these fluctuations will stop; but until they do, know that they are a routine part of healing your broken heart.

Taking Stock

Open your Heart Journal and write about the current state of your heart. Be as detailed as you can.

Exercise Review

This Phase: • Stay on top of the Nine Broken Heart Compulsive Behaviors you've identified with and work to tone them down or eliminate them entirely.
              • Add any useful quotes from this phase to your Healing Center.

Phase Two: • Repeat the First Statement of Release whenever you feel the need.

Surrender is not a passive action;

It engages the heart,

Encouraging it to stretch

Far beyond its perceived limitations.

Phase Four

The heart is fearless.

FEAR IS NEITHER a good nor bad emotion. It's intended to give you a warning, a heads-up, that something isn't right and that you might be in danger. Heartache often triggers fear because your sense of emotional safety is jeopardized. Feeling emotionally unsafe can rattle you to the core and even convince you that you'd be better off spending the rest of your life alone. While it's not always possible to stop the spread of fear, you can learn to recognize its presence and discover how to defuse it.

In this phase we'll look at the types of fear that surface with a broken heart. It might seem that fear would be the last emotion you'd have to contend with, but it can be attached to nearly everything you're thinking and feeling. The more understanding you have about what is worrying, concerning and disturbing you, the better. We'll begin our look at heartache-induced fears with the fear that you may never see your ex again.

What If We Never See Each Other Again?

When a relationship fails we're thrown into a black-and-white world that forces us to view everything in absolutes and extremes. We speak in a language inundated with razor-sharp differences, nonnegotiable choices, ultimatums and anger. We can panic, succumb to fear and anxiety, and emotionally hyperventilate in our loss. We worry that we won't be able to get on with our life. We wonder how we'll live without him, what if this is really the end, what if we've lost her forever, and what if we never see each other again.

The idea of never seeing someone again can seem like an unbearably painful proposition. We usually want to believe there is a chance for some kind of future contact with our ex. This is a normal wish; but if it transforms into a fear of never seeing our ex again, we impede our healing. As the saying goes, never is a long time and in that context we assume that never seeing our ex again would devastate us, or at the very least deeply upset and disappoint us. This is really just conjecture. Worrying about how we'll manage to get through life without our ex is a question that is fundamentally unanswerable because we can't know what we have not yet experienced. It may turn out that we get through our life beautifully without having any further contact with our ex. It remains to be seen.

One of the challenges of life is learning to stay in the present instead of continually slipping into thoughts focused on the past or future. When we're present in this way it's said we are in the "Now." Since our life is only happening in the present, not in the past or future, being in the Now allows us to experience the true moments of our life, and by being present we're able to heal. It's difficult enough to remain present when we feel fine; adding emotional pain to the mix makes remaining in the present all the more complex. You're learning how to stay present and process through your heartache. The exercise from Q&A 4 where you sat and felt individual emotions and then wrote about them is a potent example of this. While doing that exercise, you naturally had thoughts about what had happened during your relationship, which now is in the past, but you primarily focused on how each of your emotions felt in the moment—and that kept you in the present.

It isn't always easy to stay present with your emotions and if you're overly concerned with the idea of not seeing your ex again, you're spending time in future-think. This increases your pain, making it more difficult for you to stay present and staying present is the only way to resolve your pain. You unintentionally create a paradox for yourself, one that will confuse—not inform—you. Whenever you find yourself in a future-think mindset, follow these two steps:

1. Remind yourself that you're devoting energy to a way of thinking that is counterproductive to your healing.

2. Since you want to heal your broken heart, bring yourself back to the present moment.

Heart wounding is healed in the Now.

Being Heard

One of the tragedies of breaking up is that we often lose the opportunity to say how we feel to the person who broke our heart. This can leave us feeling frustrated, isolated, unrecognized and potentially very angry.

Has your ex not allowed you to express your pain to him/her? Or, if he/she has, is there more you would like to say? Use this next Q&A to say *everything* you haven't been given the chance to say.

Q&A 16.

Write a letter to your ex explaining exactly what you'd like him/her to understand about how you're feeling.

It's vital you be given the opportunity to say what you need to say. The person you want to hear you may be unavailable, but expressing yourself in writing will help you heal. For the time being, keep this letter to yourself.

The heart responds to clear and loving communication.

I Want You Back!

In any given Heal Your Broken Heart workshop there were generally a few people who had absolutely no desire to reunite with their ex under any circumstances. Everyone else was at one stage or another of wanting back in. And why not? They—and maybe you—were in love with their ex and, for the most part, they didn't choose to end the relationship. If you want a reconciliation, we want to look at exactly *why* you want to get back with your ex. Simply knowing that you want back in isn't enough. We assume that our "let's get back together" thinking is love-based, but there is a possibility it's fear-based. Here are three common examples of fear-based rationales for getting back together that we can mistakenly think are about love. See if any of them match how you feel.

> *I love him/her so much that I don't know if I can*
> *live without him/her.*

> Is this love or supersized neediness? It's easy to tell the difference. Neediness feels like we'll lose nearly everything by losing our ex: our sense of self, our belief in our future, our ability to be loved and sometimes our desire to succeed. Conversely, love is designed to make us stronger, not more dependent. Which happened for you in your relationship? Did you become stronger or more dependent?

We've worked so hard at the relationship, and it seems crazy to throw it all away.

Relationships are worth fighting for, but sometimes we need to stop the fight. Equal investment in the relationship is required from both people. It may be that you worked hard from your end, while your ex was phoning in most of his/her efforts. Take a closer look at what actually played out in your relationship, not just what you've been telling yourself happened.

I made mistakes that I want to make up for and I can only do that if we get back together.

Undoubtedly, you did make mistakes in the relationship. None of us can have a relationship without making mistakes. Unintentional mistakes are part of the relationship landscape. Intentional mistakes should not be. If you intentionally made mistakes, meaning you set out to hurt your ex, you might want to apologize for doing that, but do it here first. Take a few minutes now to write that apology.

Q&A 17.

Is there another reason, other than the ones listed above, that explains why you want to get back together with your ex? If so, what is it? Or, if you relate to one or more of the previous three reasons for reconciliation, write about your reaction to those comments.

Looking at why you want back into the relationship is important. If you want to reconnect because of a fear-based reason, you won't heal your broken heart anytime soon. I hope it makes sense to you that whether or not you choose to get back with your ex, healing your heart should take precedence.

In addition to why we might want to reconcile, there is also the issue of time. People have told me that they know it's time for them to take care of themselves, and although in many ways they would prefer to be with their ex, they realize they need to heal. Then something happens. They get a text or phone call, or need to return some of their ex's belongings, and one thing leads to another. Before they know it they're back with their ex, still wounded, probably feeling like they can't help themselves and hoping it will somehow work out this time. If this or a similar scenario develops for you, here's one suggestion. Give you and your ex another eight weeks apart once you decide to try again. This might sound like an incredible amount of time to you, especially if you're anxious to return to each other's arms, but this extra time can make all the difference. Then, after the eight weeks have passed, and it still feels like the right move for *both* of you, you can give it another go.

Why wait eight long weeks? Because rushing back into a situation that is little different than it was won't help you or your ex. With enough time apart, you might come to see the relationship more clearly and that could be what helps turn everything around in the end.

My best advice is to give yourself the time you need to work on healing your heart. Give yourself the space you need to feel more centered. Give yourself a chance to truly heal.

Moving forward is good for the heart.

Passion Drive-Bys

If you live in a city where you don't need a car, your passion drive-bys would involve a subway or bus and some walking. No matter the type of transportation involved, you may be very familiar with this urge to drive by your ex's house, apartment building, or place of work.

Passion drive-bys were on our list of Nine Broken Heart Compulsive Behaviors in the last phase, so we know that if you're doing them they involve questionable choice-making on your part.

Why do a passion drive-by in the first place? What are we after? We're afraid our ex may have moved on and we're hoping to uncover definitive proof one way or the other. We hope to catch sight of him/her, but only if it can be done covertly. The last thing we want is to be caught spying—that would look needy and desperate and make us feel even worse than we already do. Our fear wants certain questions answered. Is he home? Is there a car we don't recognize in the driveway? Does anything look different about her house? Is he sitting in the garden, unshaven, gaunt and pining for us? We generally don't get our crazier questions answered, but we sometimes get answers. It's this second scenario that's dangerous for us, because we're feeling vulnerable, and seeing evidence that our ex has someone new over at her house can re-wound our already saddened and broken heart.

Q&A 18.

1. If you've done any passion drive-bys, describe what you've learned. If you were thinking of doing more of them, do you still believe that would be the best choice?

or,

2. If you've only thought about doing a passion drive-by, after reading about them, do you still want to do one? And if so, explain why.

If you've been driving by your ex's house, think about the fact that the more often you drive by, the greater your chances are of seeing something new, something that will disturb you. You'll need to decide how big you want your exposure profile to be. My suggestion is to make that profile as small as possible. One or two passion drive-bys may be relatively harmless, although you might see more on the first one than you bargained for, but doing three or more is just asking to be hurt. You've been hurt enough.

Fear is at the root of this impulse to see and learn something, *anything*! We're afraid our ex is moving on with his/her life, and seeing evidence that someone new is spending time at his/her house would be definite proof that our relationship is over. At the same time, we're looking to see if everything seems the same, that maybe there is no one new, and that might mean there is still a chance for us. Either way, we're not helping ourselves heal because we're focusing on our ex, not on ourselves.

The Age Factor

All kinds of thoughts go through our mind when our heart has been broken, including worrying about how old we are. It's hard not to care about getting older. We're all aging. We can think of this as a negative fact of life, or we can work to understand the process better. Many elements of aging are relative. Some 14-year-olds have the outlook of 30-year-olds. More than a few 40-year-olds act like 25-year-olds. Outside the physical changes we go through as we mature, everything else is in flux. Even the physical changes are not all written in stone. But we tend to think more narrowly than this. Our concerns about getting older can slam headlong into our fear of finding a new relationship. When this happens, the age factor takes a heavy toll on our sense of self and can offset our healing.

Q&A 19.

Is there an age at which you think you'll become too old to find a relationship? If so, what age is that and why does it seem so limiting to you?

Worrying about losing opportunities to find love because of our age adds to our heartbreak. It contributes to our feelings of abandonment, loneliness and sense that our situation may never change. When someone who is 32-years-old tells me they think they're over the hill, it's not hard to help him or her see that there are many more years and opportunities to come. Once they expand their outlook, life improves for them. At what age does that counsel become wrong? I don't think it ever loses its truth, no matter what age we are. Yes, as we get older, we have fewer years remaining in our lives and some things do change, but that doesn't mean it becomes less possible for us to find love. The secret is to keep an open heart.

The heart knows no age.

Is it Over?

This exercise asks you to rate your present, post-relationship point of view.

On a Scale From 1 to 10

Choose the statement that best describes how you feel about the status of your relationship with your ex.

1. The relationship is absolutely, positively over. Under no circumstances would I want it to start up again.
2. The relationship is over. I know there is no way for us to get back together.
3. The relationship is over. I know it's much better for me not to have it start up again.
4. The relationship is over. I believe we'll both be better off if we move on, although part of me still wants us to get back together.
5. The relationship is over. I just wish I could have figured out how to save it when there was still a chance.

6. The relationship is probably over. Even though I'd prefer to have it continue, I'm not going to try to get us back together.

7. The relationship feels over. I want us to get back together, but I know the chances of that happening are small.

8. The relationship feels over, but I know if we got back together my pain would go away. I'd really like to know what went wrong.

9. My ex thinks the relationship is over; but I haven't given up on it. I'm sure if we tried again we could make it work.

10. I want us to get back together, and I'm willing to do whatever it takes for that to happen.

Wherever you fall on this one to ten scale—near the top where there is firm resolve about the relationship's end, in the middle where there is softer resolve or at the end where you definitely want back in—use this information to help you understand where you are in the releasing process.

Q&A 20.

Write about your choice from the On a Scale From 1 to 10 exercise. Are you concerned or content with what your choice seems to say about you? Would you prefer it to be different? If so, which statement would you rather have represent your current state of mind and why?

Use the information in Q&As 19 and 20 to help increase your personal insight and further define your heart healing work, not as reasons to judge or condemn yourself.

Be gentle with yourself. You deserve a soft touch.

Do Something Nice for Yourself

Emotional pain is depleting; it drains you on multiple levels. To heal fully, you'll need to replenish what your emotional trauma has stripped from you. An excellent approach to this is to develop a proactive regime of regular self-nurturance. Self-nurturance is any action you take that balances, rejuvenates, soothes or connects you to yourself. You may not have thought to care for yourself in this way, but that doesn't mean you can't begin now.

Self-nurturance teaches self-love, and as we know, it's through love that you will heal. Self-nurturance will also give you strength to fight off any of the broken heart fears you may have lurking around. Every effort you make to self-nurture will help you heal.

I know how hard it can be to find the time to care for yourself, but healing fully does require a different allocation of time than you've been used to. If you need people to help out with your schedule so you can carve out some time to self-nurture, ask them to pitch in. When people know you're working to make yourself stronger and happier, they're usually willing to do their part to help.

Caring for yourself is the same as caring for your heart.

Following is a list of a dozen self-nurturing suggestions. Try several of them to get going. Experiment and discover which ones work best for you. Incorporating a self-nurturing regime into your life is one of the most significant heart-healing actions you can take.

Twelve Self-Nurturing Suggestions

1. Take a walk by yourself and instead of being stuck in your head spend time seeing what's around you.

2. If you have access to a body of water, a river, creek or even a fountain, sit near it, listen to its sounds, feel its rhythm and relax.

3. Gather some rocks, leaves or shells and put them where you can see them daily. Bringing nature into your home can be very healing.

4. Read books that inspire you. Try including favorite books from your childhood.

5. Paint a room or a wall one of your favorite colors.

6. Pick up some new bed linens so you have an inviting place to sleep, then let yourself take a nap.

7. Spend time with people who admire and love you, and spend time with people *you* admire and love.

8. Wear clothes that make you feel good.

9. Call a friend you haven't spoken to in a long time. You'll enjoy hearing his or her voice.

10. Make your living environment as inviting as you can. Pay attention to textures, scents and colors.

11. At least once a day look into a mirror and say, "I love you."

12. Remove the hard edges from your life—loud music and noise, negative people, unhealthy food, excess stress and all forms of self-medication.

If you're like most people, you don't excel at self-nurturing. Most of us feel we either don't have the time to do anything special for ourselves, or we think that taking exceptional care of ourselves is self-indulgent and selfish. We need to reprogram this thinking, update it and bring it into the 21ˢᵗ century. Self-nurturance is a non-negotiable requirement for a healthy and balanced life. It's not indulgent, selfish or silly; it's a requisite for healing. Pick at least one action per week from the list of Twelve Self-Nurturing Suggestions on the previous page, or create your own, and schedule a time to do it—no excuses! You'll be working against a long-standing pattern that will try to convince you not to nurture yourself. Learning to follow through will make all the difference for you. This is as true for men as it is for women.

To help launch your new self-nurturing program, finish the following sentence.

The self-nurturing action I commit to doing this week is:

_____.

The more often you take loving, considerate and self-thoughtful actions, the sooner you will heal. Take care of yourself. Be kind to yourself. Love yourself.

Heart Drawing No. 2

At the end of Phase One you did your first Heart Drawing. Let's do a second one now. As before, find a blank piece of paper of any size. Use pens, pencils, paints or markers—anything and everything you want to make a drawing that shows how your heart currently feels. Place your second Heart Drawing in your Healing Center.

Something to Think About

As you've seen in this phase, fear can take many forms when your heart is broken. Fear is a reaction to something either real or imagined. You can react with fear as a result of a broken heart, but that doesn't mean there is fear in your heart. The heart holds an immeasurable amount of love but not one microdot of fear. A problem only arises when fear surrounds the heart making it feel like you can't "hear" what your heart has to say.

When someone leaves you, you lose both the person and the relationship the two of you built together. This feels like a staggering amount of loss, so it's understandable why you might become susceptible to fearful thinking. You're feeling exposed and unprotected, not strong and cared for. If it were possible to hear the language of your heart at times like this, you would be calmed and you would feel love. You may not hear that voice right now, but as you continue to heal and self-nurture, that loving heart-voice will grow increasingly stronger until one day you will hear it with perfect clarity. Every heart, even when it's broken, is filled with love.

Taking Stock

I hope you're enjoying the ritual of writing your Taking Stock section in your Heart Journal. There can be a lot to say about the state of your heart as it heals. Complete this section now.

Healing your heart takes work, care and loving attention—
all that effort will give back to you in ways
you have not yet begun to imagine.
Stay the course.

Exercise Review

This Phase: • Begin your regime of self-nurturance by taking one
                  self-nurturing action at least once a week.
                • Add any useful quotes from this phase to your
                  Healing Center.

Phase Three: • Stay on top of the Nine Broken Heart Compulsive
                  Behaviors you've identified with and keep working
                  to eliminate them.

Phase Two: • Repeat the First Statement of Release whenever you
                  feel the need.

When fear speaks to the heart,
the heart does not listen.

When the heart speaks to fear,
fear cannot help but hear.

What is the message fear hears from the heart?

That without question

And with infinite constancy,

Love forgives fear.

Phase Five

Your heart belongs to you.

WE KNOW FROM the checklist of emotions in Phase One that everyone has a powerful and diverse emotional reaction to a broken heart. Some of these emotions can be short-lived, while a few burrow in, searching for a permanent home. It's this second group of more determined emotions that can develop into behavioral traps.

A behavioral trap is any emotional reaction that becomes repetitive and consuming. Behavioral traps hijack our thoughts, perpetuate our pain and keep us from healing. They create an energy that makes them feel necessary, natural and needed—none of which they are. They have their own logic, which, while flawed, sounds perfectly reasonable to us the longer we're caught in the behavioral trap mind-set. None of us volunteers to have a behavioral trap, but it's almost inevitable that a broken heart will cause us to fall into them.

Chances are you've slid into at least one behavioral trap. Many of us struggle with several of them. Learning how to recognize and then remove behavioral traps will be our focus for the next three phases. In this phase we'll look at two behavioral traps: to begin with—the most common of the broken heart behavioral traps—the internal monologue, and then the brooding emotion of blame, which destines us to make the same mistakes again and again.

Your heart is stronger than you know.

Behavioral Trap #1: Internal Monologues

What happens to you when you get mad, when someone makes you really angry? Do you fight back and stand up for yourself? Do you take whatever is dished out and retreat as quickly as you can? Do you shut down and find it impossible to respond appropriately, or do you lash out and react irrationally? Depending on the circumstances, you may not always do the same thing; but no matter what you do, once you're alone, you probably begin an internal monologue dedicated to the particulars of what just happened to you. I chose being mad as an example, but having your feelings hurt, your authority challenged, your value questioned or your heart broken are any of a number of circumstances that can set the internal monologue mechanism into motion. And what a powerful mechanism it is!

It's easy to recognize an internal monologue if we pay attention. Most of us have had many of them. By definition an internal monologue is any internal conversation that is repetitive in nature, ranting or complaining in tone and potentially compulsive (internal monologues were among the Nine Broken Heart Compulsive Behaviors we discussed in Phase Three).

Here are six examples of common broken heart internal monologues.

- You say what you wish you'd said when you and your ex last spoke.

- You say what you'd like to say if you happen to see your ex again.

- You rework what you said in a previous conversation explaining it in much more detail.

- You respond to accusations or comments your ex made or you've heard he/she has made.

- You explain what your friends have been saying about the breakup and everything that has transpired since.

- You go off on something you imagine your ex *might* say and create an entirely new conversation to fit that fantasy.

You may be having different internal monologues than these, but the common denominator of all behavioral trap internal monologues is that they produce no positive benefits and use up hours of your day. Every moment an internal monologue engages you, you're taken away from your life and your healing. Since your internal monologues won't help you heal, you'll want to know how to eliminate them.

The goal is to learn how to indentify and then stop an internal monologue while it's in progress, which allows you to change your thinking at a critical moment. Instead of going through the entire rant in your head as you have been, you consciously choose to think of something else. This seemingly small change can have a dynamic impact on the healing of your broken heart. As one workshop member said, "It wasn't until I learned about internal monologues that I realized I'd been having the same two internal conversations every day for months! It's a relief to know I can start getting them out of my head and out of my life."

The next four Q&As will help you understand more about your internal monologues so you too can get them out of your head *and* out of your life.

Q&A 21.

Complete the following two phrases by checking the boxes that best match the subjects of your current internal monologues. Feel free to add additional descriptions at the end of each group.

My internal monologues consist of me telling my ex that...

☐ he/she has hurt me so deeply I may never get over it.

☐ he/she messed everything up.

☐ I'm incredibly mad at him/her and I can't forgive him/her.

☐ if it were true that we were really in love, we'd get back together.

☐ everything we had together now feels like a lie.

☐ _____.

My internal monologues also consist of me telling myself that...

☐ I'm unbelievably stupid for having messed everything up.

☐ I'll never figure out how to have a successful relationship.

☐ I keep making the same mistakes in every relationship.

☐ if I were a better person, he/she would still be with me.

☐ I must be cursed because I can't find someone to love me.

☐ _____.

The more you understand about your internal monologues the easier it will be to tell when you're on the verge of starting one. So, in the next Q&A give as much detail as you can about what your most common internal monologues sound like.

Q&A 22.

Write down your most repetitive and familiar internal monologue.

Now write down two other internal monologues you've had.

Read over your responses. You may have made some valid points about your ex, yourself and your lost relationship, but for the most part you probably wrote a description of what is hurting you in language that makes you feel powerless.

Love embraces you without interruption.

Q&A 23.

Name the theme(s) of your internal monologues from Q&A 22. For example, if you wrote about how unfair the breakup feels to you, the theme of that internal monologue is victimization, and you may have been victimized. Or, if you wrote about how much you miss your ex, the theme of that internal monologue is loneliness. Maybe you wrote about telling your ex that he/she had no right to make a unilateral decision about the relationship by saying it was over, in which case your theme would be betrayal. Your internal monologues may be different from these examples, but they give you an idea of what we're looking for in this Q&A. The themes of your internal monologues are like signposts on your path to healing that let you know what you need to work on, release and eventually forgive.

This next Q&A adds another layer of information about your internal monologues.

Q&A 24.

Describe the elements in your internal monologues that are harmful to you.

Recognizing how truly negative and hurtful internal monologues are can help motivate you to eliminate them. Here are three easy-to-follow steps to assist you in doing just that.

Step 1: When you realize you're having an internal monologue, acknowledge that you are.

Step 2: Tell yourself you don't want to think about your ex or yourself in these negative or fantasy-driven ways anymore. Take a deep breath...

Step 3: ... and have a different kind of "conversation" by choosing something else to focus on, like a place or idea you find beautiful and comforting.

Apply these three steps every time you have an internal monologue. In time, they'll begin to vanish, and when they do, you'll be delighted by how much more relaxed and centered you feel.

Let the language of your heart become the language in your head.

Internal monologues sneak up on us. We find ourselves embroiled in them, not knowing when the last one ended or the latest one began. Before we know it, we're living inside a series of internal conversations about our ex that, at their peak, can be so consuming it usually takes our phone ringing or another person talking to us to bring us back to reality. The mental and emotional energy required to sustain this level of internal monologue is monumental, and none of it would be possible if we didn't spend so much time in our heads.

If you think about it, you probably feel you're more in your head than in your heart lately. At the best of times, most of us are more head-centric than heart-centric, more caught up in thinking and worrying and less involved in receiving and giving love. We just feel more comfortable thinking, or thinking about what we're feeling, than experiencing life from the perspective of our heart and love. When we're hurting, the affluence of emotions we have to contend with can drive us that much more into our heads. While thinking does help us process the factual elements of our broken heart, it can also sweep us up into the tumultuous reactions we're having to our pain. We get carried away by *thinking* about how we're feeling, which keeps us from dealing directly with our emotions.

The work you've done with your emotions in the previous phases has gone a long way to get you out of your head, and we want to continue that progress. Not only will this further your heart healing, it will allow you to place even more of your awareness in your heart, the seat of love.

The next step is to observe your thinking instead of just being wrapped up in it. To do this, ask yourself these three questions:

1. Am I constantly repeating the same internal monologues?

2. If so, are they helping me resolve what is troubling me?

3. If not, are they adding to my pain?

Unless your internal monologues are helping you resolve the issues that are troubling you—and I mean *really helping* you find healthy solutions to them—you're engaging in the behavioral trap of internal monologues.

When we live in the heart, we live in love.

I like to give a three-step summary to help you focus on working through your behavioral traps. The more streamlined this part of your work is, the greater success you'll have. Place the Easy Reference Guides (ERGs) you're working with in Phases Five, Six and Seven in your Healing Center. The ERG for internal monologues looks like this:

Easy Reference Guide for Removing Internal Monologues

1. Pay attention to your thinking. Learn to recognize and acknowledge when you're having an internal monologue.

2. Whenever you find yourself having an internal monologue (or beginning one), tell yourself you no longer wish to have these types of hurtful internal conversations.

3. Move your thoughts to something more pleasant, positive and affirming.

Keep working to replace your internal monologues with healthier, more productive thinking. Before long, your head will quiet down, which will help you pay more attention to your heart.

I believe we do better when we live more from our hearts and less from our heads. This doesn't mean we ignore our thoughts, we just call on our reasoning and analytical abilities after our heart has had its say. The first byproduct of this approach is that we begin living a more compassionate life. Compassion, forgiveness and understanding then inform our view of the world. When our heart has been broken, the idea of living through the heart can seem absurd, even impossible; but moving more into our heart not only helps it heal, it also allows us to live a more heart-conscious existence.

The view from the heart is like the view from the soul—
it is immeasurably better than you might imagine.

Behavioral Trap #2: Blame

You can blame yourself, you can blame your ex and you can rail against the universe, but none of this will heal your heart. Blame will only land you back into the same kind of relationship that just failed you. Blaming others is fruitless and destructive. Blaming yourself is equally defeating. Blame is the second behavioral trap.

Q&A 25.

If you know, or suspect, that you're blaming your ex for anything that has contributed to your pain, finish the following statement.

I'm holding feelings of blame toward _____
because he/she:

If you know, or suspect, that you're blaming yourself for anything that went wrong in your relationship, finish this statement.

I blame myself for the relationship not working because I:

The language people commonly use in this Q&A is not particularly pretty, nor should it be. Blame is ugly. It comes from a place of confusion and pain, so it's not going to sound nice. Realizing it sounds as negative as it does is one of the points of this exercise. Until we look head-on at how we blame, we can deceive ourselves into believing it's not such a dangerous and limiting way to think. When we look at it squarely, we begin to see how debilitating it can be.

Blame is painful. You can't bring back your ex, but you can alter your relationship to your pain. You begin this by replacing the need to blame with the understanding that your relationship played out as it did because both you and your ex made a specific series of choices. You may not like many of those choices as you look back at them, but each one was the best it could have been at the time and under the circumstances. Learn from the mistakes you feel you made and give yourself permission to move on.

Blame can make you feel that the relationship was riding on your shoulders and you should have been able to fix what wasn't working. If you'd done a better job, the two of you would still be together, or so says blame. Relationships exist when two people participate. When one person's participation is basically nonparticipation, that person causes the relationship to derail, but blaming him for not participating is pointless. That person did what he or she was able to do. Blaming her for doing or not doing something keeps you immersed in the pain you're feeling. It will not help you heal.

Blame is the mind calling the heart blind.

To help you remove any possible blame issues you may have, fill in your ex's name in the blanks below and say both statements out loud. If you can't comfortably say the second statement today, come back later and try again.

Blame Release Statements

While I assume responsibility for my actions, I fully release myself from blame in my relationship with

_____ .

While I hold _____ responsible for his/her actions during our relationship, I fully release him/her from any sense of blame.

Put a copy of the Blame Release Statements in your Healing Center and refer to them whenever feelings of blame or self-blame come up for you.

The following ERG should also go in your Healing Center. Refer to it often if blame is an issue for you.

Easy Reference Guide for Removing Blame

1. Learn to recognize when and whom you're blaming.

2. Ask yourself: "Will my blaming help me heal and move forward in my life?" If you answer no, give yourself permission to stop blaming.

3. Repeat the Blame Release Statements whenever needed.

Releasing the need to blame is one of the most influential healing tools we have. Every effort you make to rid yourself of blame will help heal your heart.

Something to Think About

Being in a behavioral trap is similar to having a bad habit, you get accustomed to living in the mindset of a given behavioral trap, and soon, it becomes part of your life. The sheer energy created by a behavioral trap can keep you locked inside of it for months. If you identified with either or both of the first two behavioral traps, let yourself work on them every day. Stay as consistent as you can and you'll succeed in removing them.

Behavioral traps feel to me like they make a tremendous amount of noise. There's the literal "mind chatter" noise of internal monologues and the deafening, noisy distraction the other behavioral traps create. All that "noise" drains your energy. You're exhausted by the sadness of your broken heart, and the energy drain brought on by behavioral traps only adds to your depleted state. But the good news is that once you're free of your behavioral traps your energy will increase along with your emotional strength.

Taking Stock

When you begin working with behavioral traps it's common to have long-forgotten emotions come to the surface, ones that are not necessarily directly connected to your current heartbreak. If this happens, be sure to write about them while you continue to document the current state of your heart in your Heart Journal.

Exercise Review

This Phase: • Post the ERGs you're working on from this phase in your Healing Center, and incorporate those steps in your daily work.
                • Pay attention to your internal monologues.
                • Repeat the Blame Release Statements when needed.
                • Add any helpful quotes from this phase to your Healing Center.

Phase Four: • Continue to take at least one self-nurturing action this week.

Phase Three: • Stay on top of the Nine Broken Heart Compulsive Behaviors you've identified with and keep working to eliminate them.

Give your heart the chance to be free—

It will grab the opportunity with such

Determination, joy and loving abandon

That to entrap it again would be

Unthinkable.

Phase Six

The heart wants every obstacle removed.

IN THIS PHASE we'll look at two more behavioral traps: first at betrayal, the dark emotion of deceit that erodes your ability to trust, and then at rejection, an emotion especially susceptible to the influences of your historical wounding. We'll also discuss relationship arcs and how they can contribute to some relationships ending.

You learned in Phase Five that suffering through the pain and confusion of any of the broken heart behavioral traps is unnecessary. In our next two phases, we'll add additional heart-strengthening information to your behavioral trap toolbox. Whichever behavioral traps you happen to identify with, remember that you're learning how to get out of them, and before long, you will.

Identifying with several behavioral traps is normal so don't worry if you see yourself in most, if not all, of them. Understanding and then addressing what is impeding your healing is what matters most. You're not weak because you're inside of several behavioral traps; you're suffering from a broken heart.

Behavioral Trap #3: Betrayal

Trust and love are woven into every significant relationship we have. When we love someone, we trust that they are being truthful with us. We do our best to speak truthfully and can only hope for the same in return.

Betrayal is a deeply wounding abuse of trust. It makes us feel stupid, duped and gullible. It decimates relationships by destroying their foundation, making the gradual reintroduction of trust a requisite for couples wishing to reconcile. Whether or not a reconciliation is in your future, coming to terms with any sense of betrayal you may feel will help heal your broken heart. Betrayal is the third behavioral trap.

If you've been betrayed, that is an unfortunate reality. Accepting this reality will let you begin to move forward. Betrayal wants you to sit down and cry for months. It wants you to react, not understand. It hopes you'll give up and give in. It might even try to convince you that you caused the betrayal in your relationship because of the kind of person you are, and that you will forever suffer for that. Turn your back on the voice of betrayal by declaring what is true.

Say (or shout!) this statement 10 times:

I FEEL BETRAYED!

I hope that felt good. Voicing how you feel is freeing. Being specific about why you feel betrayed is the next step in moving beyond betrayal. To get to the specifics of your betrayal, answer this next Q&A in as much detail as possible.

Q&A 26.

I feel betrayed by _____ because he/she:

Your language in this Q&A may have been intense, which is a response to the intensity of the emotional impact of betrayal. As you now know, getting that language out is better than keeping it bottled up inside of you.

What motivates a person to betray, deceive, lie to, withhold information from or trick you? As we've said, you may never understand what went on inside your ex's head. People betray others for many reasons. Usually the reason doesn't have anything to do directly with us. We just have to deal with the emotional fallout from that reason. At the end of the day, analyzing the *why* behind a betrayal probably won't help you. The work at hand is to recover from the betrayal and move on. Like other behavioral traps, feelings of betrayal linger long after the deception itself is revealed. When we cling to the idea that we've been betrayed, give it further life by offering it the format of internal monologues, discuss it for months with our friends and point to it as the reason everything went wrong, we will not heal. In these ways we unknowingly breathe life into the betrayal, life it previously didn't have. We prop it up, pump it up and turn it into a sort of artificial life form dedicated to hurting us. When this happens we are deep inside the betrayal behavioral trap.

Betrayal feels like something done against you. It assaults your dignity and diminishes you. If you listen to the language of betrayal, you will believe that you've been victimized. You may feel hurt, but assuming the victim's role forces you to misinterpret what betrayal is. The fact is this: the person who betrayed you was acting against himself or herself. Why is this true? Because any time one person betrays another, he or she engages in a deceitful act, and every act of deceit is first done against oneself. Anyone who has ever lied to you, has first lied to himself or herself. He has lied to himself about who he truly is. She has lied to herself about the truthfulness of her words. He has lied to himself about what is good for him. She has lied to herself about how poorly she treats herself. These lies to the self alienate people from themselves placing them in a state of self-loathing, and from that dark place of self-betrayal comes the ability to betray others.

I know when you're in the throws of feeling betrayed, this other definition of betrayal is not necessarily easy to accept. When you've been betrayed, it's difficult not to feel that the betrayal is exclusively about you. While being betrayed is a terrible experience, and you are profoundly affected by it when it happens, the act of betrayal originates in the other person's devaluation of him or herself. Keeping this in mind can help ease betrayal's grip on your heart.

The following Betrayal Statement of Acknowledgement is a proclamation of release. Say it out loud now and add it to your Healing Center.

Betrayal Statement of Acknowledgement

I'm ready to release the resentment and pain I've felt from _____'s betrayal. While I was deeply hurt by the betrayal, I accept that it couldn't have happened if _____ hadn't first betrayed himself/herself.

Betrayal is like an undertow in the ocean. If you get caught in its language you can be pulled far from your sense of self, far from your center. Betrayal will drag you off the course of your life and continue to wound and batter your heart. Refer to this section often; it can help you process through any feelings of betrayal you may have now, or discover later.

Being betrayed does not define you—how you love does.

Here's the ERG for betrayal. Add it to your Healing Center and refer to it regularly.

Easy Reference Guide for Removing Feelings of Betrayal

1. If you've been betrayed, acknowledge it.

2. Although you've been deeply affected by the betrayal, accept that the person who betrayed you was also acting against himself or herself.

3. Work with the Betrayal Statement of Acknowledgment daily.

The heart wants to release acts of betrayal.

Behavioral Trap #4: Rejection

As an earthquake crumbles buildings, a broken heart demolishes our emotional stability. When we start sifting through the debris of our heartache, many of us discover we have strong feelings of rejection. Rejection hurts because we believe it's a measurement of our value. When someone wants to be with us, we feel valued by that person and that makes us feel good. If that same person suddenly doesn't want to be with us, we feel miserable and our sense of value plummets. This thinking diminishes us and disconnects us from our heart—and we hurt more as a result. The degree to which we feel rejected is proportionate to our interpretation of what happened. Our interpretation of what happened is dependent upon the view we have of ourselves. If our self-esteem is compromised because our spirit is wounded—we now know this is common with a broken heart—our view of ourselves becomes cloudy. Feelings of rejection overwhelm us with a sense of failure, of not being valued, wanted or desired for who we are. Rejection is the fourth behavioral trap.

Rejection can start early in life. When you were growing up, did you feel less favored by one of your parents or have an older sibling frequently tell you to leave her or him alone? Were you ever not chosen to be on the best sports team, lose a school election, have a best friend turn against you or feel unwanted for some other reason? These types of experiences can make any of us feel rejected when we're young. Most of us didn't escape childhood or adolescence without feeling the sting of rejection. Since many of us are introduced to rejection early in life, some of our adult responses to it can be tainted with a degree of preadolescent thinking. This means we unknowingly try to understand an adult situation from a child's perspective. We're bound to come up short, and we do.

Although the maelstrom of preteen and teenage angst calms down as we mature, it may never completely go away. As adults, we can still be reacting with this same adolescent-inspired explanation of why we believe some people don't like us. Here are a few examples of this painful thinking. Ask yourself if, as an adult, you've ever thought any of these:

> *She doesn't think I'm funny.*
> *He thinks I'm stupid.*
> *She must think I'm a loser.*
> *I can tell by the way he looks at me that he thinks I'm fat.*

Each of these examples is rooted in the belief that we are not enough. To change this debilitating mindset we need to update our understanding of what is actually going on when we feel rejected.

As with your past heartache (remember your drawing of hearts from Phase Two?), historical rejection can resurface when it's triggered by current feelings of rejection. Your past feelings of rejection may have resurfaced in exactly this way, compounding the sense of rejection you're already experiencing from your breakup.

This next Q&A looks at your potential connection to your earlier childhood rejection. Writing about this can help you further understand why you feel the way you do. Knowing more about your emotional state will help you heal.

Q&A 27.

Describe any childhood or adolescent episodes of rejection with family, friends, school or romantic interests that you remember.

Of these episodes, which one seems the most significant to you?

Carrying the pain of earlier rejections doesn't negate the fact that you're feeling rejected now, but it can be of some help to know that you're probably doing double duty in the rejection department. No wonder you hurt like you do.

Since your heart has been broken because your ex left you, it's easy to understand why you feel rejected. Feeling rejected for several weeks is understandable, but holding onto these feelings longer can be problematic. If the rejection theme has continually replayed in your mind for over a month, you're in the rejection behavioral trap. Lets start getting you out of there by answering the next Q&A.

Q&A 28.

I feel rejected by _____ because he/she:

Read your answer out loud and then sit with how it feels. Let yourself face the emotion as you've been learning to do.

Q&A 29.

Do you see any similarities between your current feelings of rejection (Q&A 28) and the rejections you named in Q&A 27? If so, describe them.

Not seeing a connection is fine, but some people do see a connection between their earlier encounters with rejection and what they feel today. We're focusing on your current feelings, but the following Rejection Release Statements will also help you address any past rejection you may have experienced.

If rejection is an issue for you, spend a few minutes contemplating the following two Statements of Release, and then put them in your Healing Center.

Rejection Release Statements

I fully release my <u>historical</u> feelings of rejection and free my heart of them.

I fully release my <u>current</u> feelings of rejection and free my heart of them.

When feelings of rejection surface, take the opportunity to say the Rejection Release Statements. Each time you do, you directly address the issue of rejection and restructure your patterned response to it—and that will help you heal.

Relationship Arcs

People fall in, and sometimes, out of love. When someone falls out of love with us, we can mistakenly assume there is only one reason this happens and that reason is us. Whenever we boil everything down to the common denominator of "we messed up" and give no other possible explanation as to why our ex left, not only are we oversimplifying everything, we're also wrong. It's almost always true that people breakup for more than one reason.

Even if we feel we were the sole cause of our relationship's demise, our ex often offers another explanation for his/her leaving. Maybe he felt pressured because he couldn't commit to something long-term, perhaps she loves you but isn't "in love" with you anymore, or it could be that he found someone new. Whatever reason we're given, it becomes a significant piece of the information we share with our friends to let them know why our ex said he or she left us. Our ex's "reason for leaving" eventually becomes a fact, even if we don't fully believe it, because it's all we're generally given in way of an explanation.

Q&A 30.

What reason were you given for your breakup?

What reason(s) would you give?

These two answers describe what happened in your relationship based on the experience you both had. We'll call them observable causes. In addition to the observable causes, some relationships have another factor that contributes to their ending.

Once a relationship ends you can look back at the timeline it created and the events that fall on that timeline. You know when you met, had sex for the first time, were introduced to each other's parents, went on vacation together, and so on, all the way to when you broke up. Your relationship's timeline now has a beginning, middle and end. In other words, your relationship has an arc. You know this is true because your relationship ended. It reached the end of its arc.

We often believe that everything of meaning should last forever. On one hand, we know that some of the most precious moments in life are ephemeral. We accept that perfect moments come along when they do, and although we'd like them to last forever, we know they're temporary. When it comes to relationships, we have an entirely different set of expectations. We expect, even demand, that our love relationships last as long as we want them to. Not that a lifelong, balanced and loving relationship isn't highly desirable, but not every relationship is meant to be what we'd like it to be.

When a relationship reaches the end of its arc, it changes significantly. It might stop all together with both people going their separate ways, or a friendship could survive as the romantic elements drop away. In either case, the relationship as it was has changed and it no longer exists in the way it once did.

Some relationships have short arcs, others have very long ones, and there are relationship arcs of every size in between. Clinging to a relationship after it's reached the end of its arc results in our feeling exhausted, addicted, confused and in pain. If your relationship reached the end of its arc, letting go of it is the healthiest choice for you.

Q&A 31.

After reading about relationship arcs, do you feel there may have been more to your relationship ending than the observable causes? If so, how does this new information feel to you?

Perhaps you don't know for sure if your relationship reached the end of its arc, although the chances it did are quite high. This doesn't negate the fact that both you and your ex are responsible for your own actions and reactions throughout the course of your relationship.

Regardless of how long the relationship lasted, how you treated one another during it is what makes the ultimate difference. Our information about relationship arcs can help you see your relationship in a larger context, which, in addition to giving you a better perspective on things, can gradually diminish your sense of feeling rejected.

Copy the following rejection ERG and place it in your Healing Center. Refer to it often.

Easy Reference Guide for Removing Feelings of Rejection

1. Your current feelings of rejection may be compounded by your historical experiences with rejections.

2. Use the Rejection Release Statements whenever needed.

3. Consider the possibility that your relationship may have reached the end of its arc.

The heart searches for balance so it can heal.

Something to Think About

Whichever behavioral traps you happen to identify with, remember that you're not destined to live in them forever, because you're in the process of learning how to get out of them.

One of the wonders of healing from what has hurt us is that we actually grow stronger if we stay with the work. I've seen so many people come out of their heartbreak with much more clarity, internal balance and self-love than they had before their hearts were broken. Perhaps you're feeling these same types of changes taking shape in you. There is more work to do, but you are well on your way to healing your broken heart.

Taking Stock

In your Heart Journal write about any insights you've had so far about behavioral traps in addition to how your heart is feeling this week.

Exercise Review

This Phase: • Refer to the ERGs you're working with from this phase.
                 • Repeat the Betrayal Statement of Acknowledgment and the Rejection Release Statements when needed.
                 • Add any useful quotes from this phase to your Healing Center.

Phase Five: • Refer to the ERGs you're working with from this phase.
                 • Repeat the Blame Release Statements when needed.

Phase Four: • Continue to take at least one self-nurturing action this week.

Phase Three: • Stay on top of the Nine Broken Heart Compulsive Behaviors you've identified with and keep working to eliminate them.

The heart is built of song.

It sings of love at every possible moment.

We need only sit back and listen.

Love does the rest.

Phase Seven

The heart knows what the mind does not.

REGRET TELLS YOU that everything of importance lies in the past. What you said and did, what you knew and didn't know, what you overlooked or ignored, regret says *that* is what you should pay attention to. But since you can't go back and change what happened, you're stuck constantly reviewing the minute details of your relationship and breakup without reaching any resolution. This places you in the center of the uncompromising behavioral trap of regret, and in this phase we'll discuss how to get you out of it.

We'll finish up our work on behavioral traps by looking at the inappropriateness of taking revenge—an emotional response that contemplates violent retaliation, and learn how to avoid the sometimes-tempting trap of self-revenge.

Behavioral Trap #5: Regret

Regret is an emotional albatross. Getting feelings of regret in check is vital to healing your broken heart. When you live in regret you live in the past. You disconnect from your present life and reside in what might have been. "*If only* I'd seen it coming...*If only* I'd known he/she was lying...*If only* I'd said the one thing I always meant to say...*If only* I'd tried harder," the voice of regret naggingly complains. *If only* you could turn the clock back, knowing what you know now. But, that's not possible.

Regret places you in emotional limbo. You ask to change events in the past that are simply that, in the past. Your focus on the past keeps you from living in the moment, which means you're not truly living your life. Instead, you're caught in a shadow life that increasingly distances you from those around you. Regret offers no solutions; it only produces stagnation. Regret is the fifth behavioral trap.

Relationship regret generally falls into one of two categories. The first is we regret not seeing the breakup coming. If only we could have been psychic for a little while, or at the very least intuitive enough to have saved ourselves. Of course, we're all intuitive—and chances are we felt more than a few intuitive twinges on the road to our heartbreak—but our desire to believe the best about our partner persuaded us to ignore those intuitive urgings. Most people don't listen to their intuition. Regretting that we didn't listen keeps us right where we are. Learning not to regret what happened moves us forward.

Regretting our relationship mistakes is the second major form of regret. This also includes regretting what we said or didn't say during the breakup. You may believe you made mistakes in your relationship, and as we said in Phase Four, you undoubtedly did. Mistakes are part of relationships. Continually regretting your mistakes will not help you. Accepting them as part of the natural progression of life, working not to make the same ones again, and then moving on, will.

What transpires inside of relationships is filled with purpose, even when it goes directly against our image of what we think our relationship should be. That image usually leans more toward perfection than imperfection. This is where we make a fatal mistake. Imperfection is what makes relationships sustainable. Imperfection is part of being human. It's also what allows for the most evolved experiences of intimacy. Relating intimately to another person has little to do with the romanticized images many of us have in our heads. Real relationships have flaws. Discovering what those flaws are and learning how to minimize them, without blaming anyone in the process, allows us to experience the true richness of our relationship. By directly challenging your regret you will achieve this crucial healing goal. To do otherwise burdens your already heavy heart.

Q&A 32.

Mistakes happen. When you carry regret for your mistakes, you increase your pain. By naming the actions and language you define as mistakes you initiate the process of release, which then helps you get out of the regret behavioral trap. Respond to the following two statements with as much detail as possible.

The biggest mistake I made in our relationship was:

The biggest mistake _____ made in our relationship was:

Your responses may be old information to you, but read through them now without attaching judgment to them. Doing this non-judgmentally, instead of in an accusatorial way, which you may have previously done when you thought about these mistakes, begins to distance you from the regret behavioral trap. Our regret of the mistakes *we* made is what usually trips us up. The "If I'd only..." approach to living is classic regret-thinking. We each have the right to make whatever choices we do. We may decide to make different choices in the future, but what we decide to do at any given moment is, in and of itself, simply a choice. Condemning ourselves for making any choice only hurts us more. Ask yourself if you want to feel more pain. If your answer is no, eliminating your feelings of regret is a must.

Getting out of any behavioral trap requires tools. The following spoken-word tools address the issue of mistakes. As with the other tools in the book, use these often; they will help you climb out of the regret behavioral trap. First, we'll learn the Mistake Statement of Acceptance. Use it whenever you feel yourself condemning your past choices. Read it aloud several times then put it in your Healing Center for easy reference.

Mistake Statement of Acceptance

I accept that being in a relationship involves making mistakes. I accept that I made mistakes, and although I would have liked to have done better, I know I did what I was able to do at the time. I understand that living in regret will not allow me to move forward and heal my broken heart.

Read the following two statements aloud, then put them in your Healing Center. Say them frequently; their message will help you release some of what is holding you back.

Two Statements to Release Regret

I release all feelings of regret attached to the mistakes I feel I made with _____.

I release all feelings of regret attached to the mistakes I feel _____ made with me.

Now, take a deep breath and read these two statements again. Give yourself a few minutes to fully absorb their meaning. You can use the Mistake Statement of Acceptance and the Two Statements to Release Regret alone or together.

Q&A 33.

Other than the mistakes you named in Q&A 32, were there other things that happened in your relationship that you feel regretful about? If so, please describe them.

What you regret is in the past. You can apologize for what you did if you feel the need, but you can't change what happened. Accept this fact and let yourself move on. It will help heal your heart.

The heart lovingly forgives every mistake.

Regret finds a powerful ally in internal monologues, which provide a place for regret to take root and thrive. To change this, you'll want to talk to your regret-thinking. The rule of thumb is this: Whenever you have thoughts of regret, challenge those thoughts by engaging them in conversation. This will change the balance of control by putting you in a proactive stance, instead of passively letting your regret hurt you. By literally asking each regret-driven thought to defend itself, you immediately alter the pattern in which you've been caught. Your regret will answer every time.

This technique may sound unusual, but it works — so it's definitely worth trying. By using it, you consciously *listen* to your regret-thinking, instead of simply reacting to it. This lets you completely redesign the thought process that has only brought you pain. With this technique you gain a formidable healing tool.

Here's an example of how a "regret conversation" might go. You have thoughts that say: *I wish when _____ and I first met, I hadn't insisted we spend so much time together. I think we would have done better if I'd been more relaxed. Push! Push! Push! I do that in every relationship. I can't believe I did it again. I'm so incredibly stupid!*

Instead of letting this regret-thought take hold and make you feel lousy about yourself, ask it to defend itself. Say something like: "So, regret, step out here in the open for a minute, I want to ask you a question. You just told me that if I hadn't pushed so hard with my ex we might still be together. Why do you think that?"

Next, you'll hear an explanation in your head that is your regret's defense of its reasoning. Your regret might say: *You know as well as I do that you try too hard and expect too much from people when you first meet them. You're too desperate. You drove your ex away just like you drive everyone you like away.*

You'll probably buy into whatever your regret tosses at you, since its response is based on your thinking, but don't stop there. Challenge the response. If you think, for example, that you are too desperate, as our demonstration conversation has suggested, *do not* succumb to this thinking by simply accepting it. Instead, say something back to regret like: "It's true that in the past I've had a tendency to be desperate and not let things unfold naturally. That need comes from my belief that I'm not good enough to be with someone I really like, but I'm learning to change that old, wrongheaded thinking so that in the future I'll be able to relax and just enjoy the person I'm with." By challenging the negative language of your regret-thinking in this way, you redirect that energy into something positive, and eventually your regret's responses will begin to go away. Until then, each time your regret says something back to you, do your best to counter-respond. In time, you'll have the final word, and that word will be your truth.

The next Q&A will help you get started using this conversation technique by asking you to write about the ways your regret speaks to you.

Q&A 34.

Describe what your regret sounds like when you hear it talking inside your head.

The more you learn about the sound of your regret, the easier it will be for you to have conversations with it. Before long, you'll change the pattern of your regret-thinking, and that will feel amazing!

Your regret-thinking exists because you believe its message. You've been committed to its interpretation of who you are and what your life is destined to look like. When you begin to pay attention to your regret-thinking and challenge it, you switch from suffering from its painful agenda to standing up and saying, "This isn't working for me and I'm going to show you (regret) how out of sync you are with me."

Listening to your regret's reasoning is like hearing a young child explain something. There's a lot of oversimplification and plenty of repetition. Your regret will keep returning to the same arguments to support its case, and *not* because its arguments are so immaculately sound that they answer every question perfectly. When you strip away the hypnotic haze regret-thinking conjures up, you find a logic and language void of truth. Regret depends on you thinking less of yourself. When you do, you'll blindly accept whatever it tells you.

Nearly every statement your regret presents to you will be about your failings, but *you did not fail*! You might do things differently in the future; but in the relationship you're healing from, you did what you were capable of doing—which is true of your ex too.

The heart has no room for regret; it only has room for love.

In Phase Four we talked about the Now—living in the present moments of your life. Staying in the present lets you remain conscious of what has true meaning for you. It also helps starve regret by taking away its energy source. If you're only living in the present moment, you can't live with a constant eye to the past. Regret needs you to be devoted to past-think. That's where it gets its energy. Remove your focus on the past, and you take away regret's ability to survive. When you're conscious of the ongoing present moments of your life, you won't slide into thinking regretfully about the past. When you're in the present, there will be no need to return to what you've already lived. You'll be facing forward, moving into the next present moments of your life, and regret will not be a part of your emotional thinking.

But even with a strong desire to change our facing and look to our future we can still ruminate in our regret, eventually being seduced by its conviction that we have failed. We might come to believe we deserve the pain we feel as a result of our regret, making it that much harder to accept that we are meant to heal our broken heart, not suffer from it forever.

Regret clouds our thinking, convincing us to devalue ourselves, and it can paralyze our healing. Regret is draining, distracting and emotionally expensive. If you're mired in the regret behavioral trap, you may not believe you can change your regret-thinking and get free, but you can. Just keep at it.

To help motivate you, here's a short list of what regret offers you. Put this list in your Healing Center. Read it often. It will remind you that regret will never heal you. Regret will only hurt you more.

Regret...

...keeps you from healing.

...allows you to assume blame for any and all aspects of a relationship's failure.

...spreads an aura of sorrow throughout your life by forcing you to fixate on the perceived failures of your past.

...systematically removes your ability to give and receive love by gradually closing you off from the world and trapping you in a view of the past.

...tells you that no matter what you do, the mistakes and lost opportunity of your failed relationship will forever color your life.

...keeps you where you are and doesn't permit you to move forward.

Challenge regret. Stop paying the price it extracts; it's far too high. Copy the following ERG and place it in your Healing Center. Refer to it whenever you find yourself confronted with feelings of regret.

Easy Reference Guide for Removing Feelings of Regret

1. Repeat the Mistake Statement of Acceptance and the Two Statements to Release Regret whenever you start beating yourself up with regret-thinking.

2. Talk to your regret-thinking and challenge its logic.

3. Remove your regret's lifeline by staying in the present moments of your life.

The heart wants to live fully. You can help it reach that goal.

Behavioral Trap #6: Revenge

The last thing you want to do is take revenge on your ex, and hopefully this hasn't crossed your mind. However, if you're seriously considering taking some type of revenge on him/her, please hear me out. During the time I gave the Heal Your Broken Heart workshops, it was rare for someone to express a desire to physically hurt their ex or their ex's property, but it did happen. On hearing these revenge-styled proclamations, other workshop members simultaneously condemned and understood them. Many people related to the intensity of the emotion. After all, wanting to hurt someone who has hurt us is not an uncommon response. But acting on that emotion usually takes the form of language—we yell at them—and more rarely results in our keying her car or giving him a black eye.

My message about healing involves learning to release the elements in both your thinking and emotional reactions that harm you, and discovering a deeper understanding of yourself in the process. It's about the life liberated, not the life entrapped. Well before this point in the workshop, people were aware of my healing philosophy. By the time we got to revenge, those few who had expressed a desire to hurt their ex's knew their intentions would be questioned by me, since, in my view, there is no place for violence in the healing process—or anywhere else for that matter. These people chose to speak anyway, knowing that what they had to say would be heard but definitely discouraged by the group and me. Revenge is a powerful, passionate, prodding emotion. Revenge is the sixth and final behavioral trap.

The aim of taking revenge is to cause more pain. You want someone to pay for what he or she did to you, but you'll resolve nothing by causing more pain. It doesn't matter how much your ex hurt you, nothing you do in retaliation will help you heal. If you act on your revenge, you might feel a little better for a very brief time, but soon you'll feel worse than you do right now. Causing pain to your ex will keep you embroiled in your own pain. We're working to diminish that pain, not increase it. Stay away from acts of revenge and permit yourself to continue healing.

The ERG for revenge has just one point: *Don't!*

Taking revenge will re-break your heart.

The Other Face of Revenge

Although taking physical revenge on an ex is fairly uncommon, inflicting self-revenge is more pervasive. With self-revenge, you become the target of your vengeful thoughts and actions. For people who self-blame, this is an easy trap to fall into. For example, in self-revenge you might find yourself being highly critical of yourself, thinking you're a worthless failure deserving of nothing good. You could act out on your feelings of self-revenge by choosing to work too hard, not eat well, self-medicate or act cruelly toward those close to you, thereby making yourself more emotionally isolated. When you self-sabotage, you're also engaging in an act of self-revenge, whether or not you're suffering from a broken heart. Going after yourself like this is the opposite of loving yourself, and we know that without beginning to love yourself you will not be able to truly heal your broken heart.

If you discover that you're involved in acts of self-revenge, whether through the thoughts you have about yourself and/or the actions you take against your own person, self-forgiveness is the next step in healing this unhappy condition. Before you can move to self-forgiveness however, you'll want to know if you're involved in self-revenge.

To help you identify if the self-revenge behavioral trap is one you've fallen into, complete the next Q&A by choosing the questions with which you identify.

Q&A 35.

Answer yes or no to the following:

1. Do you have a history of self-sabotage?

2. If so, have you been self-sabotaging more lately?

3. Do you resist asking for help because you think you should be able to work things out yourself?

4. Do you sit with anger and let it eat away at you?

5. Do you think that most everything that goes wrong is your fault?

6. Are you resisting letting yourself heal from your broken heart?

7. Do you believe you aren't as good as other people?

8. Is there something you know you should let go of, but keep holding on to?

If you said yes to three or more of these questions, you're probably caught in the self-revenge behavioral trap. Answer the next two Q&As to help you identify more of what you've been thinking and doing.

Q&A 36.

Describe any self-revengeful thinking you engage in:

For each self-revengeful thought you've listed, write down an alternative positive thought to replace it. Here are some examples of self-revengeful thinking and some suggestions of what to think instead.

Negative: My body will never look good enough for anyone to want
            me or love me.

Positive: My size and shape are as they are meant to be at this
            moment. If I love my body as it is it will reflect that love.

Negative: It's okay if I smoke cigarettes (drink, smoke pot, etc.); it
            helps me relax, and besides, it's my body and I get to
            decide what I put in it.

Positive: It matters what I put in my body. The more I pay attention
            to this the more I will love and connect with myself.

Negative: Nothing ever goes my way; I don't want to even try anymore.

Positive: Giving up produces a lack of future options and I'm
            ready for an abundant future.

Negative: No one has ever really loved me and no one ever will.
            Who could blame them?

Positive: I am lovable, and others love me right now.

Your self-revenge thinking may sound different from these
examples, but however it sounds, I encourage you to replace it with
positive and self-supportive language. You are definitely worth the
time and effort.

Q&A 37.

Describe any self-revengeful actions in which you participate.
These types of actions generally look like self-abuse and manifest as
overindulgence, self-medication, or highly risky or dangerous behavior.

Changing anything that is hurting you makes sense, and self-
revengeful actions are hurting you—so work to change them. The
most significant step you can take at this point is to stop any self-
revengeful actions you're currently doing. Once you've done that,

you can replace them with any of the Twelve Self-Nurturing Suggestions we discussed in Phase Four. Your heart will celebrate the change.

Now that you've identified your self-revenge thinking and actions, hopefully committed to changing those thoughts to positive and self-supportive ones, and agreed to eliminate any negative, self-wounding actions you've been taking, we can incorporate the second part of the self-revenge recovery process: forgiveness.

Think about the following statement, let its message sink in and then place it in your Healing Center so you have easy access to it.

Self-Revenge Forgiveness Statement

I forgive myself for my self-revengeful thoughts and actions, and commit to replacing them with self-loving thoughts and self-nurturing actions.

Remember not to judge your past or current self-revenge thinking or actions. Now that you can see how they've hurt you, letting go of them becomes possible. Before this, if you were mired in self-revenge, you didn't realize it. With the information you now have, you can get out of the revenge behavioral trap and continue to heal your broken heart.

Easy Reference Guide for Removing Feelings of Self-Revenge

1. Work to replace self-revenge thinking with positive thoughts.

2. Strive to replace actions of self-revenge with positive, self-nurturing ones.

3. Refer to the Self-Revenge Forgiveness Statement whenever you feel the need.

The heart does not judge—the heart loves.

Behavioral Traps Wrap-Up

The behavioral traps you've identified with will require daily attention over the coming weeks. The more attention you give to dismantling a behavioral trap, the less often it will show up. Before long, it will become a memory instead of an issue. Eliminating behavioral traps requires information and tools, which you now have; a willingness to heal, which I know you have because you've made it this far in our work together; and consistent effort, which you can learn to apply every day by using the information in the last three phases. Believe in your ability to succeed. I know you can. You don't have to spend your life trapped in thinking and actions that hurt you.

To help you stay organized, check off the behavioral traps you've identified with in this next Q&A.

Q&A 38.

I recognize that I have work to do with these behavioral traps:

☐ internal monologues   ☐ rejection
☐ blame and/or self-blame   ☐ regret
☐ betrayal   ☐ revenge and/or self-revenge

It isn't uncommon for people to check all six behavioral traps. If you did, there's nothing wrong with you; you just have some work to do—and that work will help heal your broken heart. It's possible to get out of all the behavioral traps. Know that you can and will get out of yours.

Heart Drawing No. 3

This would be a perfect time to do your next heart drawing. The rules are the same: Find a blank piece of paper of any size and express in color and shape how your heart is feeling now. When you're done, place your third heart drawing in your Healing Center.

Something to Think About

I know that after completing these last three phases, people can be surprised—even overwhelmed—by the number of behavioral traps they realize they're in. Whatever the number is for you, remember that you now have the tools to work with all six of the broken heart behavioral traps and those tools will help you succeed.

Removing internal monologues, blame, betrayal, rejection, regret and revenge present a clear challenge in your efforts to heal your broken heart. It may seem that your work just became more difficult, but in truth it has become more focused. Instead of struggling inside any of the six behavioral traps without understanding what is going on, you now know how to get out of these emotional sinkholes and move on with your healing.

There is nothing so difficult that we can't find a healthy resolution to it, and that is doubly true for behavioral traps. Grant yourself permission to move out of your behavioral traps, and then give yourself the time and effort needed to heal from them. Your heart will do the rest!

Taking Stock

As before, describe in your Heart Journal how your heart is feeling along with any other thoughts you would like to add. Everything you have to say about your healing is important.

Exercise Review

This Phase: • Refer to the ERGs you're working with from this phase.
                 • Refer to the Mistake Statement of Acceptance, Two
                   Statements to Release Regret, and the Self-Revenge
                   Forgiveness Statement when needed.
                 • Add any helpful quotes from this phase to your
                   Healing Center.

Phase Six: • Refer to the ERGs you're working with from this phase.
                 • Repeat the Betrayal Statement of Acknowledgment
                   and the Rejection Release Statements when needed.

Phase Five: • Refer to the ERGs you're working with from this phase.
                 • Repeat the Blame Release Statements when needed.

Phase Four: • Self-nurture at least once this week.

Phase Three: • Stay on top of the Nine Broken Heart Compulsive
                   Behaviors you've identified with and keep working
                   to eliminate them.

Review this phase as necessary. Your work on behavioral traps
will continue as you move ahead in the book. When you feel ready,
begin Phase Eight. Congratulations for your continued commitment
to this healing process; you're doing a superb job!

One of the great illusions is that a shattered heart
Is weak and defenseless.
Truth is,
The heart is designed to be whole,
And given even the smallest chance to heal,
It responds swiftly
With grace, power and compassion.

Phase Eight

Love is not meant to be diluted, parsed, compromised or negated. It is designed to be given and received.

YOUR HEART CAN be broken in an instant, but it takes far more than an instant for it to heal. That your heart was broken is unfortunate; that you're finding a deeper awareness of yourself by understanding your pain is a fortunate byproduct of what befell you. When you uncover the full dimension of why you hurt, you learn more about who you are and what is truly important to you.

On the path to this new understanding, you're likely to experience some anger, so we'll begin this phase with a three-part approach to dealing with that emotion. You're probably not an angry person by nature, but feeling angry because your heart was broken is very common. Once you learn to express anger in a healthy way, you'll decrease its intensity, which will make everything better for you.

Many times we want an apology from our ex. Just the idea of hearing, "I'm sorry I hurt you," can calm us. We'll take a look at your potential need for an apology and see if it's impacting you. We'll also examine how lopsided relationships never work, and define the difference between loving and non-loving words and actions. But first, roll up your sleeves, put your good-girl or good-boy attitude aside and get ready to tackle your anger!

Anger

Are you mad at your ex but trying not to be? Are you mad at yourself and tired of how that feels? Are you mad at the universe for dealing you such a lousy relationship hand? Since anger is a common response to a broken heart, it's likely you're feeling some degree of it. Just how much anger are you feeling? This next Q&A can help you find out.

Q&A 39.

Tune into your anger and spend a few minutes feeling it. Remember, your anger is a natural response to your broken heart; there is no need to feel shame about your feelings.

Rate your anger's intensity by choosing one of the listed boiling points below as you answer this question:

My anger is at a _____

☐ red-hot boil

☐ high boil

☐ medium boil

☐ low boil

☐ no boil

Chances are good you checked medium boil or higher. If you checked "no boil", you obviously aren't feeling angry, and depending on your circumstances, you may not be angry. If this is true, you could discover later that you do feel some anger, and if that happens, come back and work through this section again.

Simply being angry won't solve anything for you, but it will keep you stuck where you are. We'll resolve your anger by approaching it on three fronts. The first you've just done in Q&A 39 by acknowledging that you are angry. The second entails learning more about the energy of anger. If you have a sense of the sheer force of your anger, the magnitude it can reach when you don't try to control it, you can see that knowing some of what happens with all that energy would help you learn to manage it better. The third consists of your learning the Anger Burning exercise, which will give you some options for burning off your anger.

We'll begin with the basics about anger. Acting on anger multiplies its energy. If you've ever acted out of anger, you've probably felt better because releasing some of your anger temporarily lowered the emotional pressure that had built up inside of you. When we scream, shout or verbally attack people, we feel stronger and more in control, but this does nothing to actually release our anger. While it's true that some of our anger leaves us when we explode, it does so with a boomerang-like effect. Our anger shoots out of us, circles around and climbs right back inside of us, where it begins to build again. Instead of achieving a true release we compound our problem. Have you ever noticed how your underlying anger never fully goes away, and how, given the right occasion, even someone driving rudely can launch you into a pretty good-sized rant? Go ahead, yell at the guy if you need to, only nothing will change if you do since the true source of your anger remains, which isn't the driver who just cut you off. His or her action touched a nerve, and that is what caused your reaction. What is that nerve attached to? Is it a sense of power-lessness, issues with being bullied, not feeling respected or validated, disappointments from being passed over or perhaps a sense that you've always been on the outside? Whatever this deeper and less apparent issue is, you may not have known that your anger could have its source in something that wasn't immediately obvious to you. On the contrary, you've done what seemed logical — you've reacted to the situation in front of you and unknowingly let it substitute for the actual source of your anger. By misidentifying what you're truly angry about, you gain no relief from what is bothering you and instead get caught up in something that, in truth, matters very little.

Suppressing anger is not the answer, either. Suppressed anger builds up inside of you just as improperly expressed anger does, increasing its energy over time. What's needed is a healthy, system-atic approach to diminishing your anger coupled with a clear under-standing as to the actual source of your anger.

It may not seem true, but your ex is *not* responsible for your anger. He/She may have done any number of things that made you angry, but whatever he/she did, in and of itself, does not create the anger you feel. Your emotional investment with your ex's behavior is what creates your anger. How do I know? If your ex told me that he/she was leaving me, it wouldn't bother me, since I don't have any of my ego or heart invested in him/her. You, on the other hand, have had an entirely different reaction to the same news. It's not the news itself that is so anger-producing; it's your emotional investment in that news that is. Have you ever seen two people fight in public? Their anger is obvious; you can see it, hear it and feel it. But if all you do is watch them yell at each other and then go on about your business, their anger will not affect you. Why? Because their issues are not your issues, you have no emotional investment in any of it. They fight, while you remain detached. Change this to a situation that emotionally involves you and you shift from a casual observer to an emotionally charged participant. And so it is with your feelings about your ex.

Although you're anything but a casual observer when it comes to your ex and your feelings of anger are real, I'm suggesting that you have more influence over your anger than you may have thought. You can diminish any anger you feel toward your ex, and you can start doing it today.

Unless absolutely *nothing* happened in your life before the relationship in question—not even one other relationship of any kind that could have possibly made you angry—you've been carrying some amount of anger within you. When you get angry you're reacting to whatever just hurt you *and* past experiences that have caused you pain. This is the same idea we introduced in Phase One about historical pain contributing to current wounding. We saw this phenomenon with the emotions of the behavioral traps and it happens here with anger. Sure, you're fuming mad, but the full force of your anger may not be exclusively about your ex. That's why calling the guy and screaming at him (or engaging in any other aggressive behavior) does not work...at all...*ever*! While it can be cathartic and make you feel better in the moment, it will keep you trapped in your feelings of anger. That's not a place you want to live.

What do you do to change this? Firstly, acknowledge that what has happened to you has been painful and that one of your responses to that pain is anger. Secondly, accept that some of the anger you feel may be residual anger from historical events in your life, unrelated to your ex. And thirdly, begin working with the Anger Burning exercise.

The Anger Burning exercise will show you how to safely burn off your anger's energy without hurting anyone in the process. If you've never tried this type of exercise before, you might feel self-conscious at first, but try not to let that stop you.

The exercise has three mutually reinforcing steps. Once you get into a rhythm of doing all three, you'll see how effective they are at reducing your anger.

Anger Burning Exercise

1. Mind

We'll start with your mind. Write about your anger in your Heart Journal. Write about how you feel and say whatever you need to say to and about your ex. Never send these pages to anyone; they're only for you. If the first few times you write nothing more than several pages of swear words, so be it. The important thing is to get the emotional energy of anger out of your head and on to paper.

2. Body

Before you try any of the following suggestions, spend a few minutes warming up your body by doing some light stretching and general movements.

Pile some pillows on the side of a bed or sofa. Kneel down in front of them—or sit next to them if you prefer—and connect to your anger. When you're ready, start pounding them and really go for it! You don't have to think of these pillows as literally representing your ex, just use the physical action to help release your anger toward him/her. If you feel like saying anything or making any kind of noise, go with that too. Do this until you feel yourself relax.

People with swimming pools have told me they get in the water and thrash around until they feel their anger subside. If you have access to a pool, see if the water version works for you.

If you're a reserved person, you'll need to let yourself move beyond your comfort zone. Break through your timidity! It feels great when you do.

Once you begin to let your anger out in a safe environment, it will flow naturally. Unlike anger that volcanically erupts without warning and is devoid of personal awareness, these releases are done on your terms and with your conscious agreement. That makes them healthy, balanced and extremely effective.

3. Voice

When our heart is first broken, we utter the initial sounds of pain, but gradually we silence those very natural sighs, moans and cries of anguish. We do the same with anger. Vocally expressing our anger offers us a deep, healing release, and not doing so entraps us.

One of the easiest ways to vocally express anger is to yell while you're driving. Don't yell *at* anyone, just shout into the air. Shout words or make some off-the-charts shrieks like a howling banshee—this is no time for politeness! Go for a drive on the freeway when there's not a lot of traffic, or find a secluded road and pull over to the shoulder. If you live in a city with a noisy subway system, try standing at the end of a subway platform and yelling into the wall as a train pulls into the station. Wherever you live you should be able to find a place to do this, but if not, yell into a pillow. That works too.

This exercise is safe on every level. None of the anger you release goes to your ex, even if you focus on him/her throughout.

Performing the Anger Burning exercise in triangulation will give you the most benefit. If you can, do all three steps in one session. If that's not possible, get to each one when you have time, say over the course of three consecutive days. Either version will work. Keep at this exercise for as many days as it takes for you to feel more centered and calm, it will help cool down the red-hot energy of anger.

Anger keeps the heart from healing.

We can't have a complete discussion about anger without looking at the issue of self-anger. You may be angry with your ex, but you may also be angry with yourself. If you are, you're not alone. This happens more often than you might think. The behavioral traps of blame, betrayal, rejection and regret are each potential candidates for triggering self-anger. Anything that makes you feel like you've failed can lead you into a state of self-anger. Self-judgment is the villain here. When a person self-judges, she self-incriminates, which means she is moments away from feeling anger toward herself. There is a clear difference between having an objective view of how we've acted and deciding to change our future behavior and being angry with ourselves for things we've said or done. Anger aimed at the self acts as a weapon in the same way it does when it's aimed at another person. It's self-inflicted pain. Think of that for a moment. You're working to heal your broken heart, to lighten your pain so you can feel better again. Why would you sabotage those healing efforts by being angry with yourself?

How do you know if you're angry with yourself? Look at the actions you're taking in your life. Are any of them not for your higher good? Monitor your thinking. Are you speaking to yourself in negative and incriminating language? If you can answer yes to one or both of these questions, you're expressing anger to yourself. How do you stop? To begin, don't judge yourself for having self-anger since that would be utterly counter productive. Then consider what expressed anger is. Is it loving? No, not at all. In fact, it's completely devoid of love. To eliminate anger, put love in its place. To eliminate self-anger, be loving to yourself. Each time you're good to yourself, nurture yourself and think well of yourself, you're loving you. Take loving actions toward yourself, speak lovingly to yourself and think loving thoughts about yourself—that's how to remove self-anger.

Self-love eliminates self-anger.

Looking for an Apology?

Feeling we're owed something and that we deserve some kind of recognition for what we've been through are often the driving forces behind our need for an apology. We want proof that we were wanted, and we want that proof with a side of vindication. *I was humiliated and now you should taste a little of that same medicine*, or so the thinking seems to go. We long for our ex to accept responsibility for the relationship's failure *and* for our pain. We want to win, even this small victory.

Sometimes we want an apology, but are reluctant to admit it. If we want one, we want one. No judgment required. Wanting an apology, privately or publicly delivered, is not the problem. But waiting to get one and watching time pass while we hear nothing leaves us feeling even worse than we already do.

You may certainly deserve an apology from your ex; but if you haven't received it by now, the chances of your getting one in the near future are small. Your ex may not think he did anything especially wrong. He may believe you both made major mistakes, so why should he have to apologize to you? Or perhaps she is too embarrassed to admit she made a mess of things.

There are many potential reasons for an ex not offering an apology, none of which you may ever know. Waiting for that apology, or demanding it be given, is a waste of time and energy. Better to use your time and energy to heal.

All the same, you may still be hoping to get an apology from your ex. The next Q&A asks you to write out the apology you'd like to receive. Write everything you'd like to hear from your ex. You may never hear these words, but writing them down can be helpful.

Q&A 40.

If your ex were to give you the apology of your dreams, what would it be?

Now that you've written out this apology, work to let go of your need to receive it. The truth is, not even the most stellar apology from your ex would change what has happened.

Immerse your heart in love, not need.

What Love Looks Like and What It Doesn't

One of the key lessons about love is learning how to differentiate between the real thing and its imitators. In some relationships counterfeit expressions of love masquerade as love. When this happens, we inevitably get hurt. Our hearts are more easily broken when we don't know what love looks like, because we unknowingly start to associate non-loving actions with loving ones. If we're confused about the face of love, imagine how perplexed we are about what we should expect from it. Here's an extreme example that makes the point: If you were standing in line to buy movie tickets and the guy in front of you turned around and hit you, you might sue him for assault, hit him back or ask someone to come to your aid—and there would be no doubt in your mind that he was acting aggressively toward you. But if you were in love with someone who hit you, you might still think that person loved you, especially if he professed his love to you. Does an unlawful action in one setting translate into a loving action in another? Intellectually speaking, it does not. Emotionally speaking, for some people it can. We can unintentionally apply this same confused thinking to other inappropriate behaviors. For example, we might complain about how manipulative a coworker is and be very clear that we find that behavior distasteful, while simultaneously interpreting the manipulative language of our spouse or lover as expressions of love and concern. This rationale goes something like: *It's not how it sounds; he just wants what's best for me. He says these things because he loves me.* How do any of us end up with this kind of upside-down thinking? How have some of us, perhaps many of us, become so baffled about what love is?

The answer to both these questions lies in our history with love. That history begins when we're children, is added to when we start to have friends and intensifies once we fall in love. None of us needs to be victimized by our "love history"; but as with the history of nations, if we fail to learn from what we've been through, we're destined to suffer the same mistakes again and again.

Answer the next Q&A based on your personal experiences with love, *not* on what you may understand intellectually about it.

Q&A 41.

Make a list of the words, phrases, and actions that you've accepted as expressions of love. Everything from the sweet to the more sinister qualifies. Remember not to do this from a purely mental perspective. For example, you may know that when someone is mean or even cruel to you, he or she is not expressing love. But on an emotional level, if you've accepted this kind of treatment in the past, your definition of love played a significant role in permitting that to happen. Let this Q&A help show you how you've actually been defining love. And, yes, please do this entirely without judgment.

As you read back over this list, are there any of these personal definitions of love that you would like to eliminate? If so, stay attentive to their warning signs with new people you meet. What was previously acceptable to you will feel comfortable when you encounter it again. It's easy to fall into old patterns in new relationships; but as you gain more understanding about what love is, it will become easier for you to recognize when someone is not acting lovingly toward you. That recognition will allow you to replace your old pattern with this new non-negotiable one: *Anyone who wants to be in my life must truly love me.*

The following two lists describe some of what love is and what it's not. Which descriptions do you relate to based on your experience? Do some of the negative descriptions of love resonate with you, not in the sense of what you'd like to experience, but based on what you were "taught" about love growing up? No matter what you've believed in the past, love will not hurt you. An absence of love can cause you pain, but that's because you want back what was once there.

Add these two lists to your Healing Center and refer to them over the coming months. They will help you!

What Love Looks, Feels and Sounds Like:

Love listens.

Love sees you.

Love is generous and giving.

Love recognizes what is beautiful about you.

Love feels safe.

Love is trustworthy.

Love is constant.

Love is understanding.

Love emotionally supports you.

Love lets you know you're special.

Love wants what is best for you.

Love feels expansive.

Love is caring.

Love is patient.

Love speaks positively.

Love feels freeing.

Love does what it says it will do.

Love believes in you.

What Love *Does Not* Look, Feel or Sound Like:

Love is not stingy or withholding.

Love is not impatient.

Love is not obsessive, compulsive or insistent.

Love does not hate, ridicule or humiliate.

Love does not lie or deceive.

Love does not manipulate.

Love does not demand.

Love does not feel dangerous.

Love does not act aggressively.

Love is not distant or cold.

Love is not cruel.

Love does not strike you.

Love will not diminish you.

Love does not forget what is important to you.

Love will not abandon, betray or dismiss you.

Love does not ignore you.

Love is not disrespectful.

Love will not forget you.

If you were in a relationship that made you feel any of the non-loving descriptions listed above, you were not being loved. Identifying the expressions or non-expressions of love you experienced in your relationship helps you understand your relationship more realistically. This knowledge, while sometimes painful, will help heal your broken heart.

Many people feel validated by learning that their ex, at times, acted non-lovingly toward them. Others become upset when faced with the reality that the person they were in love with wasn't treating them lovingly. During the relationship they probably knew they weren't being loved well, but having it pointed out in such clear terms upsets them. When this happens it's not uncommon for people to defend their ex's bad behavior. If you're having a similar defensive reaction, read through the What Love *Does Not* Look, Feel or Sound Like list again and hopefully you'll begin to see that none of those descriptions is worth defending on any level. You wouldn't want any of those non-loving actions in a relationship for one afternoon, let alone as an accepted part of how you're regularly treated.

Whenever you find yourself with someone who does a non-loving action in the name of love, either challenge what he or she has done, or walk away. You are the one who has the power to change this for yourself. Only accept love, nothing less.

If you let it, love will fill in every available space,
first in your heart, then in your life.

Overinvesting

Relationships are built. Everything we put into them determines what they look like and how they function. How we communicate and act, how well we listen and nurture, how much love we give and allow ourselves to receive combine to produce the architecture of our relationship in the same way that everything which is put into the structure of a house defines the architecture of that house.

A healthy relationship is not possible unless both people invest time, love and effort to make it happen. When the investment is not relatively equal, the relationship begins to show strains. Like an architectural structure that becomes stressed, it can sag on one side or collapse entirely. A common result of this type of relationship imbalance is that one person will begin to overinvest in an attempt to keep the relationship together. In the short-term this can be a realistic solution, but stretch this out over enough time, and emotional exhaustion is the inevitable and unfortunate outcome.

To see if you overinvested in your relationship, ask yourself if you consistently worked on the relationship while your ex contributed significantly less than you. If so, you probably assumed more responsibility for the health and survival of the relationship than was best for you. This type of imbalance has several possible causes. Your partner may have watched you overinvesting in the relationship and decided it was unnecessary for him to invest much at all. She may never have felt inclined to invest to the degree you did. Or perhaps your self-worth was so compromised that it motivated you to overinvest in an attempt to prove your value and worth, whether or not your beloved made this request of you. Whatever got you to the point of overinvesting, discovering how not to do it in the future will be healthier for you.

Relationships built on one-sided overinvestment are fundamentally unhealthy because they push the person who is doing all the work to the point of physical and emotional exhaustion. If overinvesting has been a problem for you, releasing your need to do so will help keep you from partnering with people who underinvest. When you change what you do, you change whom you attract. In your next relationship, whenever you feel you are overinvesting, pause and take a step back. Evaluate where and how you're doing this and make some immediate adjustments. You'll know before long if your new beloved is willing to take up the slack (many people are), or if you've been attracted to a classic underinvestor. If you find yourself with someone like this, move on.

Criticizing yourself for overinvesting in past relationships will not help you heal. Blaming yourself for compensating for your ex's lack of investment is counterproductive. You can stop this from happening again by paying attention to what you and your next beloved are doing. You don't have to be hypercritical, just honest.

Got Something in the Bank?

You know how it goes, when you're with someone long enough you start exchanging things: CDs, books, pictures, et al. Clothes get left at each other's places; you can end up with almost anything. If you've already made a unilateral decision to throw all that stuff out, sell it online or otherwise get it out of your life instead of giving it back to your ex, congratulations on making a healthy choice! Now, follow through on that choice.

What you do with your ex's belongings will impact your heart, and we want to be sure that it has a positive, not a negative, impact. You have control over this because you get to decide what happens— at least from your end. So, if you haven't decided what to do, this would be a good time to make that decision.

Ask yourself if you're holding onto your ex's stuff because it gives you an ace in the hole in case you break down and want to see him/her one more time. If your answer is yes, you're setting yourself up to potentially experience more pain, increase your internal monologues and become attached to false hope. Considering everything you've come to understand about your heartbreak, does that make sense to you?

If you need a solution, consider this one: Have a friend return the items you have, all of them, and remove this temptation from your life. Empty your ex's "stuff account." Give everything back that doesn't belong to you. Let it all go. Release the items you've been holding onto and let that help you release the need to contact your ex.

Q&A 42.

List the items you have in your possession that you know should be returned to your ex.

Now, sign off on the following statement.

Stuff Statement of Agreement

I agree to have someone else return my ex's belong-
ings to _____ so I can continue to
support my healing. If I'm unable to find anyone to
help, I'll mail everything instead.

_____Date:_____

Excellent! Stick to this agreement; it's exactly the right thing to do.

Something to Think About

Throughout the last eight phases, you've been building a repertoire of information and tools dedicated to healing your broken heart. Your heart *is* healing. Think back to how you felt when you started this book. I hope you can see that you've made great strides since then and you deserve heartfelt congratulations for your efforts so far. You're becoming an expert on your own heart and consequently an expert on yourself.

You're in the homestretch, but we have more to accomplish before your heart will begin to feel fully healed. As a reward for your hard work, do something especially nice for yourself this week. You deserve the recognition for your consistent work to heal your broken heart. You may not have thought you had it in you to make it this far, to face your pain and learn to heal it, but look where you are, on the verge of starting Phase Nine! That is a testament to how strong you truly are.

Taking Stock

Make your weekly entry in your Heart Journal now and document how your heart is feeling. Then review the material in this phase, and when you feel ready, continue on to Phase Nine.

Exercise Review

This Phase: • Work with the Anger Burning exercise. Use its three steps as often as needed.
                • Review the two lists of loving and non-loving actions.
                • Follow through on the Stuff Statement of Agreement.
                • Add any helpful quotes from this phase to your Healing Center.

Phase Seven: • Refer to the ERGs you're working with from this phase.
                • Refer to the Mistake Statement of Acceptance, Two Statements to Release Regret, and the Self-Revenge Forgiveness Statement when needed.

Phase Six: • Refer to the ERGs you're working with from this phase.
                • Repeat the Betrayal Statement of Acknowledgment and the Rejection Release Statements when needed.

Phase Five: • Refer to the ERGs you're working with from this phase.
                • Repeat the Blame Release Statements when needed.

Phase Four: • Perform at least one act of self-nurturance this week.

Phase Three: • Stay on top of the Nine Broken Heart Compulsive Behaviors you've identified with and keep working to eliminate them.

Since it is true that your heart

Speaks the language of love,

Why not let it only

Hear the words it best understands?

Phase Nine

Care for your heart.

BEFORE BEGINNING WORK on this phase, read over your previous Taking Stock sections. It can be helpful at this point to see how far you've come since beginning this work. Acknowledging your progress to date reminds you that you're definitely doing better, and one way to quantify that progress is to see that what you've written at the end of the previous eight phases has evolved. So, take a few minutes now to look over those sections.

I hope reading your Taking Stock sections was inspiring for you. You have much to be proud of and to feel good about. Every step of your progress to heal your broken heart has taken time, effort and care. We continue this same self-loving approach as we begin our final two phases.

As you've moved from phase to phase, you've been asked to release increasingly difficult attachments. Each of these releases has been crucial to your healing and moved you closer to achieving a strong, balanced and loving heart. Releasing what you no longer need remains one of our main priorities. Later in this phase you'll have the opportunity to do our final and most powerful signing off exercise.

Also in this phase we'll look at relationship patterns and talk more about forgiveness. But first, we'll take another look at self-nurturing, this time through the lens of the classic battle between self-nurturing and self-medicating.

To live within the fullness of your heart
is to live within the beauty of your soul.

Self-Nurturing vs. Self-Medicating

When our heart is broken, we're wounded and in shock. We feel unloved, disconnected and hurt. We're in desperate need of care and love. We rarely realize that we are the person who is best equipped to give ourselves the love and care we so badly need. No one can actually do this better than we can. But because we think the solution to our heartache is going to be found outside of us, we look for solace in every direction but our own. While we look, we continue to hurt, and our pain can cause us to make a series of unhealthy choices.

You've done extremely focused work to understand the pain of your broken heart, and in the process, you've learned that complete healing cannot be forced or rushed. You may also have discovered that healing takes longer than you expect it to, and because of that, feeling frustrated from time to time is natural. When you can see that you're making progress, it's easier to let go of the *this is sure taking a long time* thinking and replace it with a sense of gratitude that you're feeling better—although sometimes you'll just want to feel better *now,* not tomorrow or next week. When this happens, you'll probably want some kind of relief to help ease your frustration. Many people find that relief by self-medicating.

While self-medicating includes the use of alcohol or drugs, it also includes anything we do to distract ourselves from feeling the pain of our broken heart. Some of the less obvious versions of self-medicating are sex, gambling, shopping, overworking, overeating, overexercising, acting aggressively or sleeping excessively. Not all forms of self-medicating are equal, but they each produce two unavoidable results. One, they temporarily numb us from the stronger emotional pain in our lives, and two, they do not help us heal.

You may not think you're self-medicating, and you may not be, but consider this formula. Anytime you feel the pain of your broken heart, you'll be motivated to do *something*. When you respond by allowing yourself to feel your pain, your healing progresses. When you choose to self-medicate, your healing stalls.

If you see that you are self-medicating, you can learn to make a different choice. Otherwise, you'll probably stay with the numbing cycle of self-medication if for no other reason than it seems to help. Even with the increased understanding you have of your emotions from our work together, you can still find yourself confronted with this issue.

When you answer the next Q&A, keep in mind that self-medicating includes anything that diverts you from experiencing the discomfort of your broken heart.

Q&A 43.

If you think (or know) you self-medicate, describe what you do.

For some people, this is an easy Q&A to answer; for others it's an uncomfortable one. Easy or not, being honest about what you're doing will help you heal.

Self-medicating is seductive for the simple reason that it lives up to its claims. It works amazingly well, for a little while. Then, when its effects wear off and our pain feels more present than ever, we're forced to self-medicate again to feel better. The more we self-medicate, the longer we postpone our healing. We become caught in a cycle of hurting and medicating our hurt. Our pain stays with us because it has nowhere to go, and consequently, we feel we have no other choice but to numb it. Our pain pushes against our consciousness, asking us to recognize and heal it, but all we want to do is escape. The solution is to let ourselves feel our emotions and then to take care of ourselves, so we have a soft place to land after we process our pain.

If you've been self-medicating, this would be a good time to stop and refocus your efforts on self-nurturing. Changing your focus from self-medicating to self-nurturing requires a substantial shift in your thinking. It means you believe your healing is *the most important thing* to you and nothing that detracts or slows it down is permissible. Since you've been working with self-nurturing since Phase Four, you're well versed in what to do. Making self-nurturing a non-negotiable aspect of your life will soothe and fortify your heart.

Self-medicating blocks the heart from receiving.

Know Thy Patterns

Ever wonder why you know how to act in a relationship? Some of what you do in your relationships may be improvised, but the majority of it is based on the relationship patterns you've developed. This is a major factor in why people go from one failed relationship to another; they unknowingly reproduce their unsuccessful relationship patterns each time and repeatedly reap versions of the same failed results.

We first learn about relationships from watching our parents interact. Our parents, no matter who they are, had patterns in their relationship. We could see their patterns at work in how they spoke to each other, if and how they expressed physical affection, how well one understood the other, and if cruelty of any kind was accepted, among other things. We watched them for years and took every nuance of it in. The better example our parents set, the better chance we have of developing healthy relationship patterns of our own. This isn't to suggest that in your relationships you haven't evolved your own way of doing things, but even those choices have some relationship to what you saw in your parents' relationship.

When we look at our relationship history, we see one or more patterns emerge. These often have to do with the types of people we attract or are attracted to, what we do at different stages of relationships or what we ask of our relationships and lovers. It can be helpful to see how in a new relationship we often duplicate thinking and choice-making that has proven unsuccessful for us in the past. With this new awareness, it becomes possible for us to make different choices, those that can produce the kinds of positive results we're after.

Recognizing your patterned behavior as it has played out in your past relationships makes it easier to see why your current pain is similar to what you felt the time before, or the time before that. Another benefit to identifying your relationship patterns is that it helps you single out potentially painful situations sooner rather than later. Knowing more about how you've been hurt in the past lets you avoid similar pain-loaded relationships in the future.

Patterns are not always easy to spot, at least in our own lives. As an experiment, ask a friend if she's watched you repeatedly pick the same type of person to be with, or seen a similarity in how you react to disappointment and loss. Tell her to be honest. You might be surprised at how insightful she is.

You may be perfectly aware of your relationship patterns, or you may be confused about what they are. In either case, working through the next Q&A will be helpful.

Q&A 44.

1. In your romantic relationships are there similarities in the types of people you pick?

   yes/no/sometimes/not sure

2. What do you look for in these people?

3. Do the people you're attracted to have this quality (or qualities) once you get to know them?

   yes/no/sometimes/not sure

4. Is there a similarity in the way your relationships unfold in the end?

   yes/no/sometimes/not sure

   If so, does this happen because you make similar choices each time?

   yes/no/sometimes/not sure

   If you answered "yes" or "sometimes," can you describe those similar choices?

5. Based on what you've just learned, do you see a pattern in your relationships? If so, can you describe it?

6. If this pattern played out in the relationship you're healing from now, explain how that looked.

7. Without judging, do you think this pattern helped you?

8. If so, explain how.

9. If not, explain how it affected you.

Identifying patterned behavior is an exceptionally useful tool. It teaches you to recognize when you're repeating what doesn't work for you and lets you choose a different course. For now, understanding how your patterned responses impacted your last relationship brings a deeper appreciation of what took place. Don't slip into the blame behavior trap here. Your patterned behavior evolved over years; that you've seen what it looks like is what matters. Learning not to repeat unhealthy patterns offers you one more strategy to help you heal your broken heart.

The heart loves the pattern of love.

Triggers

You feel like you're doing fine, swimmingly even, and then you hear his name, have a chance sighting of her, or maybe he leaves you a voice mail or sends an unexpected email or text. Whatever it is, something involving your ex happens that triggers a rush of emotions and you're knocked off balance. You feel anxious, your heart pounds and you break out in a sweat as you frantically try to figure out what to do.

These emotional eruptions will predictably trigger one or more of your behavioral traps. You might be thrust into a bout of internal monologues, become caught in feelings of rejection or relive the betrayal that occurred in the relationship. Your anger might also jump into the game, adding fuel to your emotional fire. This doesn't mean you've stopped making progress, but it does mean you've been triggered. When you experience a trigger episode, try to identify the behavioral trap that has been activated and go to that section in the book. Read the text, do the exercises again, take a deep breath and know that the next time this happens, it will be less intense.

A trigger can activate at any time. You might hear a song playing in the car next to you at a stoplight and be flooded with memories and emotions the song triggers. The light turns green, the car pulls away and there you sit with your heart aching and your eyes filled with tears. Almost anything can be a trigger. Identifying what might trigger you will help you prepare for, and recover more quickly from, the inevitable pushing of these emotional buttons.

Q&A 45.

What triggers do you think you should prepare for?

Post this list in your Healing Center and become familiar with it. Whatever you can do to avoid or prepare for these triggers will help smooth your healing.

During periods of intense healing like you're in now, it's important to make your environment as "soft" as possible. All the self-nurturing suggestions we've discussed are about making your life feel more welcoming by minimizing the hard, sharp edges that surround you.

There are two remaining hard-edged areas for us to focus on. We'll call them (1) Photos, Emails and Souvenirs, and (2) Milestone Moments and Locations. If left unattended, either of these can trigger emotional reactions that can send you cascading into unnecessary sadness; but when attended to correctly, they too will help soften your emotional environment.

Photos, Emails and Souvenirs

Do you have emails and texts, photos or souvenirs from your ex? Most of us have all four. Put whatever you have that's three-dimensional in a safe box and tuck it away where you won't accidentally come across it. Then delete the emails and texts—you've already read them, you know what they say. If the photos are on your computer, burn them to a disk if you want to keep them, then delete them and put the disk in your safe box. You can get everything that's in the safe box out in a year if you need to, but not until then. In the meantime, those photos, emails, texts and souvenirs won't be lurking around waiting to trigger you. Of course, if you want to get rid of everything, you can do that, too.

Milestone Moments and Locations

In our relationships there are special days and events that stand out in our memory and are important to us. Birthdays, holidays, vacations, anniversaries, film festivals, the first time he brought you flowers or the day she said she loved you, for example. These milestone moments present a major trigger waiting to be activated.

There are also certain locations like a street, specific restaurants, the store where he bought you that wonderful gift or a favorite city you visited together can act as a milestone location and potential trigger. Any place that had special meaning qualifies.

When a milestone moment or location is triggered, it causes a resurgence of pain. It reminds us that our beloved is no longer with us to celebrate this special occasion or place. Like most triggers, we can learn to anticipate the situations or conditions that set them off. We can prepare ahead of time for the milestone moments and locations we know we're sensitive to. We can't control every moment of our life, but we can pay attention to special dates and locations and protect ourselves from being unnecessarily wounded.

The next Q&A will help you organize the dates and places that were important in your relationship. Take the time you need to complete it fully.

Q&A 46.

Name and date your milestone moments.

List your milestone locations.

Put these two lists in your Healing Center alongside the list of triggers from Q&A 45. Use these lists as a guide. Each one is another tool that can help you heal your broken heart.

Give your heart everything it needs to heal.

Forgiveness

Finding it in your heart to forgive your ex probably isn't at the top of your to-do list. You may not wish your ex ill, but forgiving him or her might seem more than you can manage at the moment. While that's perfectly understandable, starting to work on certain aspects of forgiveness now will actually help you.

Why begin this particular work now? Because with forgiveness comes release. Not to forgive means you're holding on to something.

It might be anger, blame, resentment or feelings of self-righteousness. Whatever it is, until you release it, you won't be able to forgive.

Forgiveness is first and foremost about you, not your ex. Forgiveness is initiated by you and begins with forgiving yourself. For example, if you feel a sense of failure for the relationship not working, you'll want to forgive yourself for those failings. Then, work to forgive your ex for any of his misjudgments or failings toward you. You may need to forgive your ex for lying to you, if she lied, or for cheating on you, if you think or know she cheated. You may need to forgive him for not doing what you'd hoped he would do. Forgiveness acknowledges that mistakes were made, maybe some very serious mistakes, and that you're willing to move on from them. When you forgive, you release your heart from a burden you no longer need to carry.

Most of us want to be forgiving, at least eventually. In the bigger picture, we generally want what is best for our ex, even while we can simultaneously be working through our anger and several behavioral traps. It's fine if you aren't ready to forgive your ex today, but the next two Q&As will help you lay the groundwork for forgiving yourself now, as well as your ex when you feel ready.

Q&A 47.

I would like to forgive myself for:

Read the following statement aloud and complete it with the list or sentence you wrote above.

I forgive myself for:

Wonderful—repeat this everyday for at least a week.

Q&A 48.

I would like to forgive _____ for:

Whenever you're ready, read the following statement aloud and complete it with the list or sentence you wrote above.

I forgive _____ *for:*

Repeat this every day for a week too.

If it's too early for you to forgive your ex, come back to this Q&A in three months and see how it feels then. Give yourself another three months after that if you still need more time. Wait until you feel ready; that's what will have the most meaning.

Remember our From 1 to 10 Scale in Phase Four? It's worth doing that exercise again to see if you've shifted your point of view. Go back to page 48 and do it now.

Q&A 49.

How does the choice you made in your second pass at the On a Scale From 1 to 10 exercise compare to your original choice? If there is a difference, can you explain why?

Letting go frees the heart.

Relationship Sign-Off

Phase by phase you've been learning to let go of different elements of your past relationship, and our series of sign-off exercises have helped you succeed with those releases. This final sign-off exercise keeps with our tradition of helping you let go of what you truly no longer need. By signing your name below, you give both yourself and your ex permission to release the relationship in its entirety. Continuing to hold on to the relationship or your ex will cause you more pain and keep you where you are.

Some people experience twinges of fear when they consider signing the Relationship Release statements. If this is true for you, take whatever time you need to prepare. While you're thinking about all of this, I'd like to refer you to the following paragraph about release from Phase Three.

> What you'll discover in the process, contrary to what you may have assumed, is that when you actively release your connection to someone, you aren't left floating alone in a terrifying void. Instead, letting go of what you've clung to allows something better to move in around you. We might call that something love, a feeling of safety or a clearer sense of self. Whatever the name, how you feel when you let go will surprise you and show you there is far more good to be found in releasing than in holding on.

You will feel much better, not worse, once you release what you're still holding on to. If today is too soon for you to agree to this release, come back tomorrow and see how you feel.

I recommend ritualizing this signing-off experience. For example, you could light some candles, play music and sit quietly thinking about the significance of the release you are about to participate in.

Then, after you've singed your name below, sit quietly again for several more minutes and see how you feel.

Relationship Release Statements

I give myself permission to completely let go of every element of this relationship, which also means letting go of _____. In the process of letting go, I acknowledge that no one carries the burden of what came to pass.

_____Date:_____

I give permission to _____ to completely let go of every element of this relationship, which also means letting go of me. In the process of his/her letting go, I acknowledge that no one carries the burden of what came to pass.

_____Date:_____

Placing your signature under these two statements affirms that you are prepared to let go of the relationship you spent so much time and energy trying to save. One of the first benefits of this release is that it will give you more time to do what you want. Instead of devoting your extra energy and attention to your failed relationship, you grant yourself permission to let go of it. Granting the same degree of permission to your ex is equally important, whether or not you believe he/she is still holding on.

Put these two statements in a prominent location in your Healing Center. Congratulations on taking this vital step to heal your broken heart!

Letting go opens the heart.

Something to Think About

For most of us, letting go is rarely easy, even when we know it's the right thing to do. If formally letting go of your relationship was challenging for you, please resist any desire to judge yourself. It's certainly possible that with all you've learned about yourself and your heartache in the past nine phases, you could still find it difficult to let go of the relationship that in truth is no longer there to hold on to. In a sense, we try to hold on to something that now only finds life in our memory. Clinging to it takes us out of the present moments of our life and places us in a world that no longer exists, the world our relationship once lived within. I can bring up many details from my first major relationship. The longer I dwell on that time, the more images appear, the clearer they become, and I soon feel the love that was exchanged between the two of us. That relationship ended decades ago, but the passage of those years has no impact on my ability to connect with the essence of that relationship. I don't have an emotional attachment to those memories because I let go of the relationship a long time ago. You've just created that same emotional distance from your relationship. Your memories will stay intact, but your pain will go away — and that will feel *very* good.

Taking Stock

Open your Heart Journal and make your last Taking Stock entry. When you feel ready, move on to our tenth and final phase.

Exercise Review

This Phase: • Review the self-medicating section and continue to
                 work on the list of self-nurturing suggestions you've
                 chosen to do.
                 • If needed, return to the forgiveness exercise in
                 Q&A 48 when you feel ready.
                 • Reread the Relationship Release Statements daily
                 for the next week.
                 • Add any helpful quotes from this phase to your
                 Healing Center.

Phase Eight: • Work with the Anger Burning exercise. Use its three
                 steps as often as needed.
                 • Review the two lists of loving and non-loving actions.
                 • Follow through on the Stuff Statement of Agreement.

Phase Seven: • Refer to the ERGs you're working with from this phase.
                 • Refer to the Mistake Statement of Acceptance, Two
                 Statements to Release Regret and the Self-Revenge
                 Forgiveness Statement when needed.

Phase Six: • Refer to the ERGs you're working with from this phase.
                 • Repeat the Betrayal Statement of Acknowledgment
                 and the Rejection Release Statements when needed.

Phase Five: • Refer to the ERGs you're working with from this phase.
                 • Repeat the Blame Release Statements when needed.

Whenever you touch your heart's wisdom
You simultaneously recognize your inner beauty.
This second inevitable awareness follows the first.

Accepting your inner beauty is not only permitted
It is what the heart demands;
And you know your heart has few true demands.

So please, give it this one.
The worst that can happen is
You
Will love
Yourself
More.

Phase Ten

The love we give exists forever.

EVERY ISSUE WE'VE discussed has been aimed at bringing illumination—light!—to what was previously dark, mystifying and painful to you. Through nonjudgmental self-investigation you've made daily progress in your efforts to heal your broken heart. The healing work you've completed so successfully in the previous phases can continue once you've finished this last phase. I hope over the coming weeks and months you'll keep working on the issues that are the most sensitive to you. Old issues and patterns return in waves. You may feel great for weeks and then suddenly be hit by a memory that sends you spinning off center. The difference now is that you have the information in this book to help bring you back into balance. Rely on that information and return to it often. Your heart will open more each time you do.

Concerned about the safety or sanity of opening your heart again? It's understandable that you could be, considering the amount of pain you've endured. The good news is that you are much closer to opening your heart now than you were at the beginning of Phase

One, but to guarantee your success, there are a few more topics for us to cover.

In this phase, we'll talk about what to do when an unsuspected situation upsets you, look more into why your thoughts matter, consider when to start dating again and learn why comparison shopping with relationships is a bad idea. We'll begin with one of my favorite topics: why love is never wasted.

Love Is Never Wasted

Pain of any kind can cause us to make assumptions that are more fantasy-based than reality-based. The pain of a broken heart is no exception to this tendency. Our broken heart can lead us to assume, and consequently believe, that the love we gave in our relationship, in the end, was wasted. On one level, we probably know this isn't true. On a more reactionary, emotional level we might freely accept it.

Love cannot be wasted; that would be an impossible outcome in any situation. However, if you spent months or years pouring love into the life of someone who didn't return love to you, you may feel you not only wasted precious time but that you also wasted a fair amount of love. This is an understandable but narrow view, the view we get when we exclusively look at our ego's interpretation of events. If instead we take a step back and look at the bigger picture, we see two remarkable facts about the energy of love. The first is that even when a person doesn't consciously or actively accept the love we offer him or her, as long as the love is given freely, that person is enhanced by it. The second is that the elements of our love that are not absorbed by our beloved or desired beloved, move out into the world and exist there, offering a kind of ballast to other worldly energies. There is no waste, simply a partial redistribution of the love we've given.

Love expressed with pure intent enhances people and does not fade over time. Think about this: Every thought of love, every gesture of love, every word of love you have ever given still exists. Do the people you gave your love to know that it's remained with them? Not always, but it is possible to feel the love that people have given you. Close your eyes and try this. This can take a few minutes to develop, so give it some time. Remember someone in your past who loved you. Picture them in your imagination and let their image become clear. Reconnect with the love you felt for them, and let yourself feel the love they had for you. Now, just focus on the feelings of love they felt for you. Feel that? That love is still with you. By feeling it today, you do more than conjure up its memory; you literally feel what has been with you all these years. It's as real in this moment as it was when it was first lavished upon you, no matter how the relationship ended.

Love endures. Love cannot be destroyed. You can turn your back on love, but love itself does not leave. We leave. Our emotions flee, drift off or are pushed away. Our commitment to people and relationships can dissolve, but every pure expression of love we give to others lives on. You wasted nothing by giving your love to someone, even if he or she ultimately could not accept it. Know that this is true.

Send love out into the world wildly and recklessly—
throw your head back, open your arms and let it rip!

Sign-Off Overview

You've done an immense amount of work to heal your broken heart. One look at your Healing Center and Heart Journal makes this clear. Reviewing everything you signed off on or agreed to in the last nine phases gives another powerful example of what you've accomplished. Here is that remarkable collection of self-loving proclamations.

Phase One: You acknowledged that your heart was broken and you wanted to heal it.

Phase Two: You released your need to understand your ex's logic and agreed to stop listening to music that could increase your sadness.

Phase Three: You named the person who broke your heart.

Phase Five: You assumed responsibility for your actions and released yourself from blame — and you did the same for your ex.

Phase Six: You released yourself from the pain of betrayal. You released any need you may have had to feel rejected.

Phase Seven: You agreed to release any feelings of regret surrounding the mistakes you feel you made in your relationship. You agreed to the same for your ex.

              You forgave yourself for any feeling of self-revenge you may have had.

Phase Eight: You worked to release the anger that has been holding you back.

Phase Nine: You granted both yourself and your ex permission to let go of the relationship.

These were powerful, deep and courageous releases. Bravo to you for all that exceptional, loving work!

Love heals the heart.

You did your first Heart Drawing in Phase One and your second and third in Phases Four and Seven. As we complete our work, this would be a natural time to do your final Heart Drawing.

Heart Drawing No. 4

For your final Heart Drawing, I'd like you to make a collage. A collage is a collection of images on a chosen topic or theme. Traditionally, pictures are glued to a common surface like a large piece of heavyweight paper, cardboard or canvas, but use any surface you like. A three-dimensional collage is also an option. The size of your collage is entirely up to you.

Remember, this is about expressing yourself emotionally in another form than the written or spoken word. Collect images and colors that represent the current state of your heart and combine them in any way you want.

Think of this as an emotional exercise, not an intellectual one. In other words, don't predetermine how you feel. Instead, look through magazines, newspapers, postcards or flyers—any sources you can find—and put whatever you relate to in your collage. Stay open to surprises!

When you've finished your collage put it with your other Heart Drawings in your Healing Center and move on to the next Q&A.

Q&A 50.

Compare your four heart drawings and describe their similarities and differences.

Your Heart Drawings provide a vivid visual example of the road you've traveled to heal your broken heart. I hope seeing them together brings you joy. Your heart is no longer as it was; it will forever be stronger and more secure as you move forward in your life.

Why Your Thoughts Matter

When we discussed internal monologues in Phase Five, we said that what goes on in our head affects how we feel. What we repetitively think we eventually manifest, in one way or another. Having the occasional odd thought generally has no real impact on us; it's what we think on a regular basis that colors, shapes and influences our lives.

The mind is busy and often surprisingly redundant. We'll pick one or two thought-themes and return to them every chance we get. A person whose thought-themes swing to the negative throughout the day is having a very different life experience than someone whose thought-themes are creative, loving, inspiring and filled with possibilities. This positive approach by no means rules out being practical; it simply rules out living in a negative mindset.

You had your heart torn apart. It's not that easy to lift your chin up and head back out into the fray with your mind suddenly filled with positive I'm-a-wonderful-human-being kinds of thoughts, even after all the work we've done. But you can make your reentry a little easier by staying attentive to your thinking. For example, throughout the day, check in with yourself to see if you're thinking like one of your behavioral traps. If you are, you're having less than supportive thoughts about yourself. Instead of judging yourself for these thoughts, redesign your thinking. In Phase Seven you learned to have a conversation with your negative thinking, challenge it and replace it with a positive alternative. You can do a shorter version of that technique by monitoring your thinking and replacing any old and unwanted thoughts with new ones. Following are three examples of how this might work. No matter which version of negative thinking you come up with, find a reasonable and positive thought to offer as a counter response.

Loving thoughts help the heart heal.

Replace: I'll never find someone to love me.
With: I will find the right person to love me. I just haven't
           found him/her yet.

Replace: Every time I try to love somebody I get hurt. I just don't
           think I can love someone again.
With: Getting hurt in relationships happens. Everyone experi-
           ences it. I deserve to be loved again and I will be.

Replace: Everyone else seems to have such great relationships.
           There must be something wrong with me because I keep
           ending up alone.
With: What is healthy, balanced and loving for me can start
           entering my life today. I accept this to be true.

Redesigning your thinking is one of the most influential daily exercises you can perform.

Getting Back in the Game

If you've been healing a recently broken heart, as opposed to one from your past, you'll eventually want to start dating again, find a new relationship and try your hand at love again. What you've learned about your heart, relationship patterns and the behavioral traps you are susceptible to, will help you as you move forward. If you apply what you've learned from our work together, your future relationship experiences can be different. The question is, when do you get back in the game?

When our heart has been broken, people want us romantically involved again as quickly as possible. Getting back into the dating world makes sense, but doing it too soon can feel disorienting. In a very real way, you may have only recently begun to feel less trapped in your emotional fetal position. This is a major shift, and it will take time for you to adjust to your new emotional legs. Give yourself time to make this adjustment, remain sensitive to your own rhythm and honor your own timing. That's how you'll know when dating again is right for you. There is no need to rush, no matter what anyone says.

If you want to start dating and you feel ready, give it a go. If things don't go well at first, take a little more time off and then try again. Your goal is not to find the love of your life in the next person you meet, it's to meet new people and allow yourself to open up to fresh possibilities. It's not always easy to reenter the dating scene. Take the time you need and know that when you first start seeing people again it doesn't have to go perfectly. Do what feels comfortable for you, listen to your heart and you'll do fine.

Relationships are not science, so let your heart lead the way, not your head.

Comparison Shopping

When you meet someone new, and you will, you can expect to do a certain amount of comparing, but recognizing exactly what it is you're comparing can make all the difference for you. If you catch yourself comparing your new date with your ex, ask yourself if the comparison feels like loss. For example, say you spend some time with Mitch and you think to yourself: *Mitch seems like a nice guy, but he doesn't make me laugh like Charlie did.* On the surface this is probably an accurate and unbiased observation, but deeper down you might actually be thinking something more like, *I'm still hurting from not being with Charlie, and here's just another example of how no one will ever be like him.* There is a world of difference between these two thoughts. In the first, you think you're only commenting on Mitch's beige sense of humor, but when you look more deeply, you see that you're viewing Mitch through the filter of your loss.

When we assess anyone from a place of loss, that assessment has loss written all over it. If Mitch asks you out to dinner, and as you look across the table at him, you see how he's not like your beloved ex Charlie, you see what Mitch is not—not who Mitch is. In other words, if you're motivated from an emotional place of loss, loss is what you'll see sitting across from you, not the person who asked you out on a date.

Comparing can easily develop into judgment, and judgment is a synonym for pain. Comparing can therefore become an expression of pain. Making casual comparisons is natural. Your ex had brown hair, and this new person is a blonde, for example. But when comparing is an expression of your loss it interferes with the forward progression of your life.

The next Q&A looks at the issue of comparison. The information you gain from it can help save you from future heartache.

Q&A 51.

Are there qualities or attributes your ex possessed that you might use to negatively compare against someone new? If so, please list them.

Refer to this Q&A when you start dating again. Remember that comparing anyone new to your ex, other than the casual comparisons already mentioned, will keep you from discovering who any new person is, and probably just make you feel disappointed in him or her. This is not the way to find a new relationship, because you're still investing in the old one.

If you find that you can't stop comparing, after trying not to, it may be a sign that it's too soon for you to start dating, so give yourself a little more time.

Attempting to love again can feel like you're entering into scary and dangerous territory. To help you get over this understandable reentry hurtle, try using the following affirmation daily.

It's safe for me to love again.

Say this affirmation often. Before you know it, you might begin to believe it's true (because it is!). That belief will help you love again.

The love that is in you has always been with you.
It can only increase in volume, beauty and depth.

Rings Around Your Heart

I know from having given the Heal Your Broken Heart workshops and from my private practice that the tools and information you've been given in this book can heal your heart, no matter what the circumstances of your relationship were or the particulars of your life situation are. You only have to keep up the work you've so successfully completed to this point. What you may not have realized is that every effort you've made since beginning Phase One has helped draw a series of concentric rings around your heart. Each of these rings makes you stronger, more emotionally aware and better able to be in the world as the loving person you are.

Depending on your point of view, this idea could sound either reasonable or bizarre. Whichever it is for you is fine, of course, although if you side with the more bizarre view, consider opening yourself to the poetry held within these heart rings. Our hearts relate to lyrics and poetry, and perhaps your heart will relate to what follows.

Here's how these seven healing rings were placed:

> Ring No. 1 was placed in Phase One when you acknowledged that you didn't want to continue hurting in the ways you had been.

> Ring No. 2 was placed in Phase Two when you released the need to understand your ex's logic.

> Ring No. 3 was placed in Phase Three when you began working with the Nine Broken Heart Compulsive Behaviors.

> Ring No. 4 was placed in Phase Four when you seriously began to self-nurture.

> Ring No. 5 was placed by your dealing directly with your behavioral traps in Phases Five, Six and Seven.

> Ring No. 6 was placed by completing the Heart Drawing exercises.

> Ring No. 7 was placed in Phase Nine when you signed the Relationship Release Statements.

These seven energetic rings will remain around your heart. Whenever you listen to your heart and act upon its guidance you'll reinforce these healing heart rings. Think of them as real or imaginary — either way is fine — but from time to time, remember to think of them.

Let your heart be a beacon of love.

In Phase Two we discussed how having a broken heart wounds our spirit, and you did a multiple-choice Q&A that looked at the state of your spirit. That Q&A is worth doing again to help you see how you've progressed. As before, pick the response to each question that most closely matches how you're feeling now.

Q&A 6. (revisited)

1. How emotionally stable do you feel right now?

☐ very ☐ somewhat ☐ not at all

2. How hopeful do you feel about your life in general?

☐ very ☐ somewhat ☐ not at all

3. How hopeful do you feel about your ability to love again?

☐ very ☐ somewhat ☐ not at all

4. How hopeful do you feel about your ability *to be* loved again?

☐ very ☐ somewhat ☐ not at all

5. How possible do you feel it is to recover from your current feelings of loss?

☐ very ☐ somewhat ☐ not at all

6. How positive do you feel about your relationship future?

☐ very ☐ somewhat ☐ not at all

7. How positive do you feel about your future in general?

☐ very ☐ somewhat ☐ not at all

8. How strong does your spirit feel?

☐ very ☐ somewhat ☐ not at all

I know that by repeating this Q&A that you've just *seen* what you've been *feeling*: That on a core level you have truly begun to heal.

Your heart shines.

Look Into Your Eyes

One of the expressions of the emotional fetal position is that we see sadness in our eyes. It's likely you saw sadness in your eyes when we originally talked about this. Look in the mirror again now and see how your eyes look to you today. There may still be some sadness there—that wouldn't be uncommon at this point—but you may very well see quite a difference from before.

This is a good exercise to do from time to time. Look into your eyes and see what's there. You're either out or nearly out of your emotional fetal position, and your eyes will reflect this lighter, more positive feeling. The better you feel, the softer your eyes will become. Never judge what you see when you look into your own eyes, and instead use that "window to your soul" (and heart) as a source of personal guidance and love.

We've reached our final Q&A. As with our other Q&As I hope this one adds to your personal insight and understanding. Not everyone believes life is filled with lessons, but I think it's hard not to see a lesson in how our relationships play out. See if you can name your life lesson in our last Q&A.

Q&A 52.

Describe the lesson you believe you are meant to learn from your relationship.

Whatever that lesson is, do your best to learn it, that way you won't have to repeat it again. That's the perfect preventive measure.

Reminders

You've completed the majority of your work to heal your broken heart, but there are a few points to keep in mind over the coming weeks. Here's a list to help you stay organized in your follow-up work.

1. If you wrote an apology in Phase Four for any intentional mistakes you may have made in your relationship, reread it now. You may not need to send it, but if you feel you want to, consider waiting another three months before you do.

2. Review the Exercise Review section at the end of Phase Nine, and continue the work you have in place from the previous phase until it's completed.

3. Keep your Healing Center up for six more months. Continue to add to it as you move forward. Use it as your visual diary, your healing road map, and a continual source of guidance and inspiration.

4. Remember the drawing you did in Phase Two of your other broken hearts? When you're ready, consider going back through the book to heal the broken hearts represented in that drawing. If there are more broken hearts than you can consider mending, pick three or four major ones. This means going through the entire process with each of those broken hearts individually—it's well worth the effort.

5. Things to think about *in three months*: (1) Is this a better time to work on forgiving your ex as addressed in Q&A 48 in Phase Nine? (2) Consider retaking the On a Scale from 1 to 10 exercise in Phase Four. (3) Does it still feel like you need to send that Phase Four letter?

Final Thoughts

The more secure you feel in your ability to nurture and love yourself, the easier it will become for you to recognize the love that is all around you. If love is the answer, as I believe it is, and your heart is the energetic channel for the expression of love, it stands to reason that caring for yourself—and thereby caring for your heart—helps bring "the answer" of love more vividly into your life.

Congratulations on all the work you have put into this process, on allowing yourself to learn more about who you are and on having the courage to face what has been hurting you. Reward yourself with a heart-gift: something simple and lovely that will help you remember all the progress you've made. Use the new energy you've gained throughout this healing process to help you get excited about life again; let it be the fuel that propels you forward.

Each time I guide someone through this process, I marvel at the amazing odyssey we take into his or her interior landscape. I feel extremely fortunate to have seen as many beautiful hearts as I have, even while the owners of those hearts thought theirs were deficient, unreachable and beyond repair, as you too may have felt. Consider how much better you understand your heart now than you did when you started this book. You have grown within your knowledge of who you are and what is truly important to you. Take that knowledge and apply it to your life.

Your healing efforts will continue to be rewarded and reflected back to you every day. You are beginning a renewed life experience. Your heart can now shine forth into your life and into the lives of everyone you know. Thank you for opening your heart.

Your heart is the ocean of your being.
It is deep and wide
And will accommodate countless ships
Sailing the world of you.

Your heart is the ocean of your being.
Its waves caress you,
Reminding you that if you need to touch shore
You will be guided to those golden sands.

Your heart is the ocean of your being.
Its spray will cleanse and refresh you
Every day
Of your life's journey.

Your heart is the ocean of your being.
What you used to think was small and frail
Was actually a steadfast friend in disguise.
Tear off that disguise, see through the camouflage,
Embrace that old friend who is you.

Your heart is the ocean of your being.
Go crazy and jump in!

How amazing it is to feel the heart within itself again.
How wonderful to know you have regained what felt
Lost to you.

How remarkable to see your internal aperture shift
So magnificently
To perfectly accommodate the light
Now streaming effortlessly from within you.

Your heart knows more about love

Than every other part of you combined.

So, do what's natural!

Express your heart's expertise

Courageously and continuously.

Give and receive

Love

Lavishly!

For More Information

Visit me on the Heal Your Broken Heart blog on my website at www.michaelkane.org—where I talk more about healing, answer reader questions, and keep you updated about the book. Just click on the *Heal Your Broken Heart* book icon anywhere in my site and join in the conversation. I'd love to hear from you!

You can also join me on Facebook at *Heal Your Broken with Michael Kane* or follow me on Twitter *@kanemichael*.

To email me directly, visit the Contact page on my website or write *michael@michaelkane.org*.

About the Author

Los Angeles based life consultant Michael Kane has earned a reputation as a compassionate and inspiring advisor and teacher for his seamless blending of the pragmatic and the intuitive. Over the past twenty years he has helped hundreds of people find a deeper connection to self-awareness and love through his private practice, workshops and lectures.

www.ingramcontent.com/pod-product-compliance
Lightning Source LLC
Chambersburg PA
CBHW031339040426
42443CB00006B/392